International Law: A Handbook for Judges

By David J. Bederman

*with Christopher J. Borgen
and
David A. Martin*

Under the auspices of
the Judicial Outreach Program of
The American Society of International Law

Studies in Transnational Legal Policy • No. 35
The American Society of International Law
Washington, DC

ISBN:0-9729423-4-3

Subscription Information

Studies in Transnational Legal Policy is the occasional paper series of the American Society of International Law. Standing orders may be placed with the Society. As new issues become available, persons with standing orders will automatically receive the issue and be billed accordingly. The price of each issue will depend on the length of the particular study.

For the current price list and information on back issues, please contact the American Society of International Law, 2223 Massachusetts Avenue, NW, Washington, DC 20008-2864; telephone (202) 939-6000; fax (202) 797-7133.

> **Authorization to photocopy** items for internal or personal use (beyond that permitted by Sections 107 and 108 of the U.S. Copyright Law), or for the internal or personal use of specific clients, is granted by the American Society of International Law for users registered with the Copyright Clearance Center (CCC) Transactional Reporting Service, provided that the base fee of $10.00, plus 25¢ per page is paid directly to CCC, 222 Rosewood Drive, Danvers, MA 01923. For those organizations that have been granted a photocopy license by CCC, a separate system of payment has been arranged. The fee code for users of the Transactional Reporting Service is: 1057-0551/94 $10.00 + .25. Educational copying is permitted. Please address requests to CCC Academic Permission Service: (508) 750-8400; fax (508) 750-4744.

©2001 FOUNDATION PRESS
©2003 THE AMERICAN SOCIETY OF INTERNATIONAL LAW
Printed by Cadmus-Port City Press Division, Baltimore, MD 21208

TABLE OF CONTENTS

ACKNOWLEDGMENTS xi

ABOUT THE AUTHORS xv

ABOUT THE ASIL xvii

FOREWORD xix

INTRODUCTION 1
   A. What Constitutes "International Law?" 2
   B. A Summary of U.S. Constitutional Provisions Concerning International Law 4
      1. Role of Treaties in U.S. Law 4
         a. Article VI, Section 2 4
      2. Presidential Powers 4
         a. Article II, Section 2, Clause 2 4
         b. Article II, Section 3 4
      3. Congressional Powers 4
         a. Article I, Section 8, Clause 3 4
         b. Article I, Section 8, Clause 10 4
      4. Judicial Powers 5
         a. Article VI, Section 2 5
         b. Article III, Section 2 5
      5. Federal States 5
         a. Article 1, Section 10, Clause 1 5
         b. Article 1, Section 10, Clause 3 5

C. The Role of Treaties and Customary International Law in U.S. Law 5

D. Examples of International Law Interacting with U.S. Domestic Law 7
    1. Alien Tort Statute 7
    2. Anti-Terrorism Legislation 8
    3. Trade-related Disputes 8

E. An Introduction to International Courts and Tribunals 10
    1. The Proliferation of International Courts and Tribunals 10
    2. No *Stare Decisis* (but precedential weight) 12

I. A BRIEF HISTORY OF INTERNATIONAL LAW 13

A. From Westphalia to World War Two: 1648–1939 13

B. From the Second World War to the Post–Cold War World: 1939 to the Present Day 14

II. SOURCES OF INTERNATIONAL LAW 17

A. Treaties and Other International Agreements 18
    1. General Features 18
        a. Introduction 18
        b. Bilateral and multilateral treaties 19
        c. Reservations 20
        d. Default rules 20
    2. Treaty Interpretation 21
        a. Basic Rules 21
        b. Schools of Interpretation 21
            i. Textualist 22
            ii. Intentionalist 22
            iii. Teleological 23
    3. Suspension and Termination of Treaties 24
        a. Breach 24

   b. Fundamental change 25
   c. Preserving obligations in cases of hostilities . 26

B. Customary International Law 26
  1. Formation of Customary International Law 26
   a. General practice 27
   b. Accepted as law 27
  2. Discerning Whether Customary International
   Law Exists in a Particular Case 27
  3. Opting out of a Customary Norm 30
  4. Conflicts Between a Treaty and Customary
   International Law 30

C. General Principles of Law 31
  1. Effects of Domestic Law on International
   Law 31
  2. U.S. Practice 33

**D. Other Sources and Evidence of International
  Law** 33
  1. Case Law of Courts and Tribunals 33
  2. Teachings of Highly Qualified Publicists 34
  3. Equitable Principles 34
  4. The Role of General Assembly Resolutions 36

III. PUBLIC INTERNATIONAL LAW AND U.S. LAW 39

**A. The Interrelationship of International Law
  and Domestic Law** 39
  1. Introduction: Monism and Dualism 39
  2. International Law and the Constitution 40
   a. Domestic effects of international law 40
   b. International obligation 41
  3. The Role of Customary International Law 42
  4. Customary International Law and
   Federalism 43
  5. Customary International Law and Federal
   Statutes 44

B. Treaties and the Laws of the United States 46
    1. The Treaty Power 46
        a. Constitutional provisions 46
        b. "Advice and Consent" and RUDs 46
        c. Constitutional limitations on the Treaty
           Power 47
           i. The Bill of Rights 47
           ii. Federalism 47
           iii. Rejected theories of limitation 49
    2. Judicial Enforcement of Treaties 50
        a. Self-executing and non–self-executing
           treaties 50
           i. The question of self-execution of a
              treaty 50
           ii. Private rights of action 52
           iii. Application 52
        b. The Last-in-Time Rule 53
           i. Later Treaty/Earlier Statute 53
           ii. Later Statute/Earlier Treaty 54
           iii. Qualifications to application of the
              rule 54
        c. Treaty termination issues 55
    3. Executive Agreements 56
        a. Congressional-Executive Agreements 56
        b. Sole Executive Agreement 57

IV. SUBJECTS OF INTERNATIONAL LAW 61

    A. States 61
        1. State Identity, Recognition, and Succession 61
           a. The elements of statehood 61
           b. Recognition 63
              i. The politics of recognition 63
              ii. Consequences of non-recognition 63
           c. State succession 65
              i. Defined 65
              ii. Legal Effects 66

    2. State Responsibility 67
       a. Defined 67
       b. Main issues 68
          i. Admissibility 68
          ii. Attribution 70
          iii. Wrongfulness 71

B. International Organizations and Tribunals 72
    1. The League of Nations and the United
       Nations 72
    2. Specialized Agencies and Regional
       Institutions 73
    3. The International Court of Justice 74
       a. Historical Background 75
       b. Structure 75
       c. Operating procedures 76
          i. Jurisdiction by compromis or
              compromissory clause 77
          ii. Compulsory jurisdiction 78
          iii. Findings of inadmissibility 78
          iv. Provisional measures 79
          v. Advisory opinions 80

C. Individuals as Subjects of International Law ... 80
    1. Nationality 81
       a. Bases 81
       b. Statelessness 81
       c. Dual Nationality 82
       d. Tension between nationality and rights ... 82
    2. Duties of Persons under International Law
       and International Criminal Law 83

V. Substantive Issues 87

A. Human Rights 87
    1. The Universal Declaration 87
       a. Background 87
       b. Nonbinding 89
       c. Evolution of norms 89

    2. Other Global Instruments 89
        a. Binding instruments 89
        b. The United States and the ICCPR 90
        c. Issue-specific conventions 91
    3. Regional Human Rights Systems 92
    4. Derogation 93
    5. The Customary International Law of Human
       Rights 94
        a. General examples 94
        b. The Alien Tort Statute and the Torture
           Victim Protection Act 94

**B. The Law of War and International Humanitarian
Law** 96
    1. Introduction 96
    2. The Hague Law 96
    3. The Geneva Conventions 98
    4. Treatment of Enemy Nationals 100

C. International Economic Law 100
    1. International Trade and Monetary Law 101
        a. Friendship, commerce, and navigation
           treaties 101
        b. The Bretton Woods institutions,
           generally 101
        c. The GATT, the WTO, and NAFTA 102
        d. The IMF 104
    2. International Development and
       Investment 104
        a. Investment protection 104
        b. Dispute resolution and ICSID 105

D. The Law of International Common Spaces 105
    1. Law of the Sea 106
        a. Internal Waters (IW) 107
        b. Territorial Seas (TS) 107
        c. Contiguous Zones (CZ) 108

       d. Continental Shelves (CS) and Exclusive
          Economic Zones (EEZ) 109
       e. High Seas (HS) 109
   2. International Environmental Law 111
       a. Relation to state responsibility 111
       b. Examples of international environmental
          regulation 112
       c. Relation to international trade law 113

E. Immigration and Citizenship 115
   1. Overview 115
       a. International framework 115
       b. U.S. legal framework 117
       c. U.S. agencies 119
   2. The Application of Human Rights Norms 120
       a. Nondiscrimination 121
       b. Family life 122
       c. Detention 123
       d. Immigration procedures 124
   3. Refugee Protections 125
       a. Convention and Protocol Relating to
          the Status of Refugees 125
       b. Convention Against Torture 128

BIBLIOGRAPHY 131

ACKNOWLEDGMENTS

Although there are just three authors listed on the title page, this *Handbook* is the result of the efforts of many people working together under the auspices of the American Society of International Law's Judicial Outreach Program. In particular, this *Handbook* is the result of the leadership of Justice Sandra Day O'Connor, the chairperson of the Advisory Board of the Judicial Outreach Program. Justice O'Connor was the motivating force behind the organization and completion of this project. Her commitment to increasing the breadth and depth of understanding of international law by the American bench has both defined and energized the *Handbook*.

Another board member who made this project possible is Rita Hauser, President of the Hauser Foundation. The first four years of the Judicial Outreach Program, including the production of this *Handbook*, was made possible in large part by a generous grant from the Hauser Foundation. But beyond financial assistance, Rita Hauser was one of the original planners of the Judicial Outreach Program, defining its goals, scope, and programs along with Justice O'Connor and Professor Thomas Franck of New York University's School of Law, who was then President of the ASIL. Together they built the foundations of the program of which this *Handbook* is only part.

We have been fortunate to have an advisory board whose members have taken the time to be active participants in this project by reviewing drafts, providing guidance and suggestions, and pointing out areas needing further work. Besides Justice O'Connor and Rita Hauser, Advisory Board members during the writing and editing process were:

The Honorable Juan R. Torruella
United States Court of Appeals for the First Circuit

The Honorable John M. Walker
United States Court of Appeals for the Second Circuit

The Honorable Edward Becker
United States Court of Appeals for the Third Circuit

The Honorable J. Harvie Wilkinson
United States Court of Appeals for the Fourth Circuit

The Honorable Carolyn Dineen King
United States Court of Appeals for the Fifth Circuit

The Honorable Boyce F. Martin, Jr.
United States Court of Appeals for the Sixth Circuit

The Honorable Margaret Daughtrey
United States Court of Appeals for the Sixth Circuit

The Honorable Diane P. Wood
United States Court of Appeals for the Seventh Circuit

The Honorable Roger L. Wollman
United States Court of Appeals for the Eighth Circuit

The Honorable M. Margaret McKeown
United States Court of Appeals for the Ninth Circuit

The Honorable Robert H. Henry
United States Court of Appeals for the Tenth Circuit

The Honorable Rosemary Barkett
United States Court of Appeals for the Eleventh Circuit

The Honorable Harry T. Edwards
United States Court of Appeals for the District of Columbia Circuit

The Honorable Fern M. Smith
United States District Court for the Northern District of California

Thomas Franck
NYU School of Law and ASIL Past President

Arthur Rovine
Baker & McKenzie and ASIL Past President

Anne-Marie Slaughter
ASIL President and Dean, Woodrow Wilson School, Princeton University

Charlotte Ku
ASIL Executive Director and Executive Vice President

Judge Rosemary Barkett and Judge Robert Henry must be particularly noted for volunteering to undertake extra editorial reviews of drafts. Judge Barkett could have been listed as a co-author of this *Handbook*; her substantive comments, suggested text, and formatting and organizational advice profoundly affected the final version of the text. Judge Robert Henry also provided excellent guidance in his memoranda and suggestions, pointing out issues that we had not previously considered. We thank them for their energy and commitment to this project.

Advisory Board members Thomas Franck, Arthur Rovine, Anne-Marie Slaughter, and Charlotte Ku and ASIL members Carlos Vazquez of Georgetown University Law Center, Rick Kirgis of Washington and Lee University School of Law, Andrew Vollmer of Wilmer, Cutler & Pickering, and Harold Hongju Koh of Yale Law School also provided close readings and detailed substantive comments of drafts of this *Handbook*. Their contributions added depth and accuracy to the text.

John Cook and Mira Gur-Arie of the Federal Judicial Center also provided many helpful comments on an early draft of this *Handbook*. We are indebted to them.

Mieke Clincy of the ASIL staff provided copyediting that involved excellent substantive comments, revisions, and line-edits. Her careful review has made this *Handbook* not only more readable, but more useful. Although this project began prior to Kathleen Wilson's tenure as ASIL Director of Research and Outreach, it was completed under her guidance. Kathleen's skillful management of the final editing process and her insightful substantive contributions were of significant importance to this *Handbook*.

We could not have asked for a better team to work with.

Finally, we would like to note that portions of this *Handbook* have been drawn from INTERNATIONAL LAW FRAMEWORKS by David Bederman, published in 2001 by Foundation Press.

David J. Bederman
Christopher J. Borgen
David A. Martin

About the Authors

David J. Bederman is Professor of Law at Emory University School of Law in Atlanta, Georgia.

Christopher J. Borgen is Assistant Professor of Law at St. John's University School of Law in New York City.

David A. Martin is the Warner-Booker Distinguished Professor of International Law at the University of Virginia Law School.

ABOUT THE ASIL

The American Society of International Law (ASIL) is a nonpartisan membership association committed to the study and use of law in international affairs. Organized in 1906, the ASIL is a tax-exempt, non-profit corporation headquartered in Tillar House on Sheridan Circle in Washington, DC.

For nearly a century, the ASIL has served as a meeting place and research center for scholars, officials, practicing lawyers, judges, policy-makers, students, and others interested in the use and development of international law and institutions in international relations. Outreach to the public on general issues of international law is a major goal of the ASIL. As a nonpartisan association, the ASIL is open to all points of view in its endeavors. The ASIL holds its Annual Meeting each spring, and sponsors other meetings both in the United States and abroad. The ASIL publishes a record of the Annual Meeting in its *Proceedings*, and disseminates reports and records of sponsored meetings through other ASIL publications. Society publications include the *American Journal of International Law*, *International Legal Materials*, the *ASIL Newsletter*, the ASIL occasional paper series, *Studies in Transnational Legal Policy*, and books published under ASIL auspices.

The ASIL draws its 4000 members from nearly 100 countries. Membership is open to all—lawyers and non-lawyers regardless of nationality—who are interested in the rule of law in world affairs. For information on the ASIL and its activities, please visit the ASIL Web site at <http://www.asil.org>.

Foreword

By Sandra Day O'Connor
Associate Justice, Supreme Court of the United States

This overview of international law should provide much-needed background in an area of the law that is rapidly emerging in ways that affect courts here and abroad. The reason for the expanded focus on international law, of course, is globalization. No institution of government can afford now to ignore the rest of the world. The importance of globalization should not be underestimated. Thirty percent of our gross domestic product is internationally derived. We operate today under a large array of international agreements and organizations: the UN Convention on Contracts for the International Sale of Goods, NAFTA, the World Trade Organization, the Hague Conventions on Collection of Evidence Abroad and on Service of Process, and the New York Convention on Enforcement of Arbitral Awards, to mention only a few. But globalization is much more than simply these agreements and organizations. Globalization also represents a greater awareness of, and access to, peoples and places far different from our own. The fates of nations are more closely intertwined than ever before, and we are more acutely aware of the connections. As we learned in this country on September 11, 2001, these connections can sometimes be devastating rather than constructive. But as we also are learning in the post–September 11 world, the power of international cooperation and international understanding is much greater than the obstacles we face.

The word "globalization" has many connotations, some positive and some negative. The varying views on the subject are reflective of both the potential of globalization to increase world harmony, and the risk that globalization will suppress desirable differences and become simply a tool for imposing the preferences of powerful nations like our own upon the rest of the world. Harnessing the good that can come from our increasingly global world while avoiding its pitfalls requires those with power and influence in our country to develop a greater knowledge and understanding of what is happening outside our nation's borders.

This is true of courts and of lawyers as much as it is of relevant governmental bodies. There is talk today about the "internationalization of legal relations." We are already seeing an increase in international law issues in American courts. This does not mean, of course, that our courts can or should abandon their character as domestic institutions. Very few treaties are directly enforceable in American courts. But international law is no longer confined in relevance to a few treaties and international business agreements. Although international law and the law of other nations are rarely binding upon our decisions, conclusions reached by other countries and by the international community should at times constitute persuasive background in American courts.

The Court on which I sit held almost 200 years ago that Acts of Congress should be construed to be consistent with international law absent clear expression to the contrary.[†] Somewhat surprisingly, however, this doctrine is rarely utilized in the Court's contemporary jurisprudence. I can think of only two

---

[†] Murray v. Schooner Charming Betsy, 2 Cranch 64 (1804).

cases during my now more than 20 years on the Court that have relied upon this interpretive principle.††

The fact is that international and foreign law are being raised in our courts more often and in more areas than our courts have the knowledge and experience to handle comfortably. There is a great need for expanded knowledge in this field. And the need is now.

International law is the expression of agreement on basic principles of relations between nations. It is a factor or a force in gaining a greater consensus among *all* nations, and it can be and is a help in our search for a more peaceful world. Our efforts, both in the United States and abroad, to educate law students, lawyers, and judges about international law are efforts well spent.

Kofi Annan has said: "The rule of law is essential to peace, development and the realization of human rights. The practice of law is a privilege, but a privilege that carries with it a heavy responsibility to ensure respect for the law."††† American judges are becoming more aware of their responsibilities to respect not only domestic law, but the law of nations as well. Because of the scope of the problems we face, understanding international law is no longer just a legal specialty; it is becoming a duty common to judges and lawyers alike. I believe this brief *Handbook* published by the American Society of International Law will provide a clear and readable introduction to some basic concepts of international law for the benefit of both the bench and the bar.

---

†† Weinberger v. Rossi, 456 U.S. 25 (1982); Trans World Airlines v. Franklin Mint, 466 U.S. 243, 252 (1984).
††† Kofi A. Annan, *Guest Foreword, in* GLOBAL LAW IN PRACTICE, at v, v–vi (1997).

INTERNATIONAL LAW: A HANDBOOK FOR JUDGES

INTRODUCTION

This *Handbook* is intended to provide a starting point for understanding the relationship between international law and U.S. law, and the ways in which international law is applied in the United States. It includes discussion of U.S. constitutional provisions and certain U.S. statutes relating to international law, as well as an introduction to the history, sources, and interpretation of international law and its primary "subjects": states,[1] international institutions, and individuals. The *Handbook* will also identify the various international courts that apply international law and their relationship to and impact upon U.S. law and courts. Finally, the *Handbook* will review a handful of substantive international law doctrines related to human rights, the law of war, international economic law, the law of international common spaces, and the regulation of immigration and citizenship.

Material has been selected for this *Handbook* with a particular eye to problems and issues that federal judges may confront when rules of international law become relevant to disputes and cases decided in the United States. As such, the *Handbook* is not a

---

[1] In international law, the term "state" normally refers to a country or nation-state. For purposes of this *Handbook*, states within a federal system, such as the United States, will be distinguished as "sub-federal entities" or "federal states."

comprehensive treatise on international law; rather, it is designed to provide an overview of selected topics and to guide the reader to sources for further research. (While the text of this *Handbook* is lightly footnoted for readability, key sources are documented and a selected Bibliography is included at the end.) Other useful works for general international law research include the American Law Institute's *Restatement (Third) of the Foreign Relations Law of the United States (Restatement)*,[2] and the *ASIL Guide to Electronic Resources in International Law*, available both in book form and on the internet, <www.asil.org/resource/home.htm>.

The remainder of this introduction provides a thumbnail sketch of relevant constitutional and international legal provisions, examples of certain key U.S. statutory provisions relating to international law on a variety of issues, and an introduction to international courts and tribunals.

A. What Constitutes "International Law?"

The term "international law" has been used at various times to describe different things. This *Handbook* will focus on what is known as *public international law*—"the law which regulates the intercourse of

---

[2] RESTATEMENT (THIRD) OF THE FOREIGN RELATIONS LAW OF THE UNITED STATES (1987).The *Restatement* describes the "foreign relations law" of the United States as

international law as it applies to the United States; and

domestic law that has substantial significance for the foreign relations of the United States or has other substantial consequences.

RESTATEMENT § 1.

nations."[3] Generally speaking, however, "international law" also refers to laws and choice-of-law rules that govern the cross-border activities of individuals, corporations and other private entities—traditionally known as *private international law*. In addition, the term "international law" is also used in some contexts to refer to *foreign law*—i.e., the domestic laws of other nations—as well as *comparative law*, which involves the study and comparison of different legal systems.

The disciplines of public international law, private international law, and comparative law are overlapping to a greater and greater extent.[4] At the same time, the building blocks of international law, broadly understood, include a wide range of activities and regimes beyond treaties, such as domestic statutes with extraterritorial application, the transnational coordination of regulatory agencies, and the treatment of aliens by foreign governments.

In sum, today's lawyer is increasingly involved in what some commentators have called *transnational law*, a term coined by Phillip Jessup "to include all law which regulates actions or events that transcend national frontiers."[5] At issue is not simply the law of interstate relations or the law of international business transactions or comparative law, but also the web of legal regimes between and within countries that is the result of globalization.

---

[3] BLACK'S LAW DICTIONARY 733 (5th ed. 1979).
[4] *See, e.g.*, ANDREAS LOWENFELD, INTERNATIONAL LITIGATION AND ARBITRATION 5 (1993) (stating that "in many ways the barriers between public and private international law have broken down, and the overlap or gray areas between public and private law, and public and private international law continue to grow").
[5] PHILLIP C. JESSUP, TRANSNATIONAL LAW 2 (1956).

B. A Summary of U.S. Constitutional Provisions Concerning International Law

1. Role of Treaties in U.S. Law

a. Article VI, Section 2: This Constitution, and the Laws of the United States which shall be made in Pursuance thereof; and all Treaties made, or which shall be made, under the Authority of the United States, shall be the supreme Law of the Land . . . .

2. Presidential Powers

a. Article II, Section 2, Clause 2: [The President] shall have Power, by and with the Advice and Consent of the Senate, to make Treaties, provided two thirds of the Senators present concur; and he shall nominate, and by and with the Advice and Consent of the Senate, shall appoint Ambassadors . . . .

b. Article II, Section 3: [The President] . . . shall receive Ambassadors and other public Ministers . . . .

3. Congressional Powers

a. Article I, Section 8, Clause 3: [The Congress shall have Power . . .] to regulate Commerce with foreign Nations . . . .

b. Article I, Section 8, Clause 10: [The Congress shall have Power . . .] to define and punish Piracies and Felonies committed on the High Seas, and Offenses against the Law of Nations.

4. Judicial Powers

a. Article VI, Section 2: This Constitution, and the Laws of the United States which shall be made in Pursuance thereof; and all Treaties made, or which shall be made, under the Authority of the United States, shall be the supreme Law of the Land; and the Judges in every State shall be bound thereby, any Thing in the Constitution or Laws of any State to the contrary notwithstanding.

b. Article III, Section 2: The judicial Power shall extend to all Cases, in Law and Equity, arising under this Constitution, the Laws of the United States, and Treaties made, or which shall be made, under their Authority;—to all Cases affecting Ambassadors, other public Ministers and Consuls; to all Cases of admiralty and maritime jurisdiction . . . and between a State, or the Citizens thereof, and foreign States, Citizens or Subjects.

5. Federal States

a. Article 1, Section 10, Clause 1: No State shall enter into any Treaty, Alliance, or Confederation . . . .

b. Article 1, Section 10, Clause 3: No State shall, without the Consent of Congress . . . enter into any Agreement or Compact . . . with a foreign Power . . . .

C. The Role of Treaties and Customary International Law in U.S. Law

As noted above, the Constitution provides that treaties are part of the supreme law of the land and Congress is able to define and punish violations of the law of nations. Treaties are unambiguously part of federal law, although questions can arise as to whether a particular treaty or parts of a treaty are "self-executing," or whether additional action by Congress is required for domestic effect. Treaties supersede all inconsistent state law, notwithstanding the lack of participation by the House of Representatives in their making.[6]

Whereas the status of treaties is specifically delineated in Article VI of the Constitution, the role of "customary international law"—discussed at length in section III below—is not mentioned. Consequently, the role of customary international law vis-à-vis U.S. law has been questioned periodically by various commentators. Most U.S. courts and commentators, nevertheless, treat customary international law as federal law. In cases where questions are raised of what is or is not international law, it is the responsibility of judges in the United States to ascertain international law and to apply it.[7]

As discussed further in section III.A.2, for purposes of U.S. law, the Constitution supersedes any conflicting provision of international law, just as it supersedes any conflicting federal statute. As expressed by the authors of the *Restatement,* "[i]n their character as law of the United States, rules of international law

---

[6] *See, e.g.,* Ware v. Hylton, 3 U.S. (3 Dall.) 199, 236–37 (1796).

[7] *See* The Paquete Habana, 175 U.S. 677 (1900) ("International Law is part of our law and must be ascertained and administered by the courts of justice of appropriate jurisdiction as often as questions of right depending upon it are duly presented for their determination"); *see also* RESTATEMENT, *supra* note 2, § 113, cmt. b, "Judicial notice of international law" (stating that "[t]he determination of international law or the interpretation of an agreement is a question of law for the court, not a question of fact for a jury").

and provisions of international agreements of the United States are subject to the Bill of Rights and other prohibitions, restrictions, and requirements of the Constitution, and cannot be given effect in violation of them."[8] (As explained in section III.A.2, for purposes of international law, the fact that a particular provision of a treaty or customary international law is inconsistent with the U.S. Constitution does not necessarily relieve the United States of any corresponding international obligation.)

When there is a conflict between a treaty and a federal statute, the later in time prevails as a matter of U.S. law,[9] as explained below in section III.B.2. Similarly, conflicts between treaty and custom can be resolved by applying various criteria such as the existence of peremptory norms, denunciation provisions in the treaty, and the intent of the parties, as discussed in section II.B.4, below. Most U.S. courts and commentators at present do not accept customary international law as taking precedence over a contrary statute or treaty.

D. Examples of International Law Interacting with U.S. Domestic Law

1. Alien Tort Statute

In 1789, the first Congress provided that U.S. courts would have "jurisdiction of any civil action by an alien, for a tort committed in violation of the Law of Nations or a treaty of the United States."[10]

---

[8] RESTATEMENT, *supra* note 2, § 111, cmt. a, "International law and agreements subject to the Constitution."
[9] *See, e.g.*, Whitney v. Robertson, 124 U.S. 190, 194 (1888).
[10] 28 U.S.C. §1350 (2003).

2. Anti-Terrorism Legislation

The United States is party to ten international conventions that are explicitly focused on combatting terrorism.[11] Each convention criminalizes a specific act or acts, and requires all treaty parties (known as "states parties") to a) make such offenses punishable; b) "prosecute or extradite" suspected offenders; and c) provide assistance to prosecuting states. Each of these conventions was given domestic effect in the United States through the passage of specific implementing legislation.[12]

3. Trade-related Disputes

The law of international trade and finance has a wide variety of effects on domestic law. At the most basic level, tariff levels are normally set in conformity with General Agreement on Tariffs and Trade/World Trade Organization (GATT/WTO) requirements.

---

[11] Other treaties/conventions may have the suppression of terrorism as one of their goals or effects, but as of January 2003, these ten multilateral conventions are those generally referred to as the "Terrorism Conventions."

[12] The ten conventions and their implementing statutes are: The Hague Convention on the Unlawful Seizure of Aircraft—49 U.S.C. §§46501-02 (2003); The Montreal Convention (aviation sabotage, including bombing)—18 U.S.C. §31–32, 49 U.S.C. §46501 (2003); The Convention on the Prevention and Punishment of Crimes Against Internationally Protected Persons (diplomatic security)—18 U.S.C. §§112, 878, 1116, & 1201(e) (2003); Nuclear Materials Convention (covering unlawful taking of nuclear material)—18 U.S.C. §831 (2003); Hostages Convention—18 U.S.C. §1203 (2003); Airports Protocol to the Montreal Convention—18 U.S.C. §37 (2003); Unlawful Acts Against Maritime Navigation—18 U.S.C. §2280 (2003); Fixed Platforms—18 U.S.C. §2281 (2003); Suppression of Terrorist Bombings—Public Law 107–197 (June 25, 2002); Suppression of Terrorist Financing—Public Law 107–197 (June 25, 2002).

But the law of international trade has begun having an impact on a wider variety of cases through various dispute resolution procedures.

The WTO dispute resolution mechanism allows states parties to file suits against one another for any breach of one of the WTO agreements, such as the GATT. Recent cases have dealt with issues with broader policy impacts such as whether U.S. regulations requiring "dolphin-safe" methods of catching tuna fish to be sold in the United States were impermissible under WTO guidelines.[13]

Another form of dispute resolution is the investor-state dispute resolution allowed under Chapter 11 of North American Free Trade Agreement (NAFTA) and various bilateral investment treaties (BITs). NAFTA Chapter 11, for example, allows the national of a state party to seek recourse against another state party before the International Centre for the Settlement of Investment Disputes (ICSID) or similar arbitral forum for a claim based on the investment protection measures of NAFTA.[14] Such cases are relatively new, and the effects have yet to be fully weighed; recent arbitral cases filed by foreign nationals against the U.S. government have dealt with issues ranging from whether the level of punitive damages awarded by a Mississippi jury, and Mississippi's appeals bond requirement, denied the Canadian judgment-debtor fair and equitable treatment under international law to whether a California state regulation banning a gasoline additive

---

[13] 30 I.L.M. 1594 (1991); 38 I.L.M. 118, 174 (1999).
[14] North American Free Trade Agreement, Dec. 17, 1992, ch. 11, art. 1120, 1992 WL 812394. ICSID was established by the Convention on the Settlement of Investment Disputes Between States and Nationals of Other States, Mar. 18, 1965, 17 U.S.T. 1270, 575 U.N.T.S. 159.

caused an unjust expropriation of profits from a Canadian company.[15]

E. An Introduction to International Courts and Tribunals

1. The Proliferation of International Courts and Tribunals

The International Court of Justice (ICJ)—at times called the "World Court"[16]—is one of the better-known international courts, and has decided a broad range of cases and issues. However, there have also been many lesser-known specialized international tribunals in modern history.[17] Examples include international claims tribunals, which for over 200 years have settled financial and property disputes between countries, and international criminal courts, including the Nuremberg tribunal after World War II and more recent institutions for the former Yugoslavia and Rwanda. After the Second World War there also developed human rights commissions and courts such as the Inter-American Commission on Human Rights

---

[15] For a list of cases being heard under the auspices of ICSID (though not necessarily arising out of NAFTA), see *ICSID List of Last Pending Cases, available at* <www.worldbank.org/icsid/cases/pending.htm>.

[16] This is a term used for both the Permanent Court of International Justice of the League of Nations and the International Court of Justice of the United Nations. See section IV.B, below.

[17] For analytic charts describing international courts and tribunals, see generally the website of the Project on International Courts and tribunals, <www.pict-pcti.org>, and in particular the "Synoptic Chart" at <www.pict-pcti.org/publications/synoptic_chart.html> and the "Research Matrix" at <www.pict-pcti.org/matrix/Matrix-main.html>.

(in which the United States participates) and the Inter-American Court of Human Rights (whose jurisdiction the United States does not accept). There are also economic and trade institutions (including the European Union, NAFTA, and WTO) that have associated judicial bodies to resolve disputes. In general, there has also been a trend toward both an increasing number of international tribunals, and an increasing use of each tribunal; consequently, there has also been a significant expansion of international case law.[18]

Some tribunals—including, for example, the ICJ, the International Tribunal for the Law of the Sea, and the Inter-American Court of Human Rights—are empowered to render advisory opinions interpreting certain aspects of international law. With respect to disputes between two or more parties, there are a number of tribunals, such as the World Court, which accept only claims between states. Others allow individuals and other "subnational actors" to have standing before them. U.S. courts may interact with international tribunals in a variety of ways, ranging from enforcing awards to referring to the decisions of these tribunals on a point of law. The relationship of U.S. courts to the ICJ has been highlighted in a series of recent cases related to the detention of foreign nationals in the

---

[18] *See generally* Cesare P.R. Romano, *The Proliferation of International Judicial Bodies: The Pieces of the Puzzle*, 31 N.Y.U. J. INT'L L. & POL. 709 (1999); Jonathan I. Charney, *Is International Law Threatened by Multiple International Tribunals?*, in 271 RECUEIL DES COURS 101 (1998). *See also* Jonathan I. Charney, *The Impact on the International Legal System of the Growth of International Courts and Tribunals*, 31 N.Y.U. J. INT'L L. & POL. 697 (1999); *Developments in International Criminal Law*, 93 AM. J. INT'L L. 1 (1999).

United States and the application of the Vienna Convention on Consular Relations.[19]

2. No *Stare Decisis* (but precedential weight)

As a legal matter, decisions of these tribunals do not generally constitute binding precedent, even for the tribunal that issued the decision. In this respect, international tribunals resemble more closely civil law jurisdictions (such as those that dominate in continental Europe) where the doctrine of *stare decisis* does not exist. Indeed, Article 59 of the ICJ Statute says emphatically that, except as between the parties to a dispute, a decision of the World Court has no binding effect. As a practical matter, however, international tribunals almost invariably follow their precedents, especially on procedural issues. It is furthermore routine for international lawyers to rely heavily on prior judicial decisions to support their arguments. International tribunals (as well as domestic courts considering international law issues) thus make use of previous decisional rulings on relevant issues. At the same time, it would be a mistake to assume that an international tribunal (just like a domestic court) is obliged to follow its precedents.

---

[19] *See* Federal Republic of Germany v. United States, 526 U.S. 111 (1999) and the related ICJ decision, LaGrand Case (F.R.G. v. U.S.), 1999 I.C.J. 9. *See also* Breard v. Greene, 523 U.S. 371 (1998) and the related ICJ decision, Case Concerning the Vienna Convention on Consular Relations (Para. v. U.S.), 1998 I.C.J. 248.

I. A Brief History of International Law

A. From Westphalia to World War Two: 1648–1939

The date that is commonly given as the birth of modern international law is one of European origin. It is 1648, when a comprehensive peace treaty, the Peace of Westphalia, ended the Thirty Years' War—a ferocious and bloody religious conflict in Europe. The Peace of Westphalia, signed by virtually all European nations, exemplifies two significant characteristics of the development of international law.

The first is that international law needs states in order to function. But more than that, it needs states with strong internal institutions and cohesion. We would recognize these traits today as sovereignty and nationalism. The notion of sovereignty—and its handmaiden of *positivism* (the idea that states are subject to no legal authority above them)—had not always been the dominant theory of international law (and indeed, is under challenge today). In Europe during the Middle Ages, for example, international law was instead seen as an outgrowth of universal values and norms, largely derived from Roman law (the *jus gentium*, which applied to all peoples, and the *jus civile*, or civil law), religious institutions (the law of the Roman Catholic Church, or canon law), and common European customs involving such transnational issues as trade and control of conflict (the *jus commune*).

The second phenomenon heralded by the 1648 Peace of Westphalia is that the defining moments for international law of the last three and a half centuries have followed periods of intense global conflict. New international organizations, new substantive rules of international conduct, and new procedures of dispute settlement between international actors, for example, were part of the peace settlements ending several cataclysmic wars: the 1763 Definitive Peace (concluding the Seven Years War or Great War for Empire), the 1815 Final Act at Vienna (ending the Wars of the French Revolution and Napoleon, 1791–1815), the 1919 Treaty of Versailles and Covenant of the League of Nations (completing the First World War, 1914–18), and the 1945 Charter of the United Nations (marking the end of World War II, 1939–45).

B. From the Second World War to the Post–Cold War World: 1939 to the Present Day

The cataclysm of the Second World War remade the globe. First, it accelerated the process of decolonization. The British and French colonial empires collapsed by the early 1960s, and by the 1980s there remained no part of the world that was under forced colonial domination. This meant that the international community—the family of nations—grew into a large, diverse group. Before 1945, the group of "civilized" nations had never numbered more than fifty. By 1960, it had increased to a hundred, and, in the year 2003, it had grown to about 195 states. The sheer increase in the number of states (quite apart from other international actors) has changed the face of international law in fundamental and irreversible ways.

World War II and the Cold War rivalry that followed also set in motion a host of technological, social, environmental, and economic phenomena that we now identify as "globalization." Whether it is the integrated international economy and trade disciplines, nuclear power and proliferation, space exploration and computer applications, environmental pollution and habitat degradation, or intellectual properties and entertainment, we are gradually living in a shrinking, interdependent world. International law has been compelled to respond to these functional demands of the international community.

At the same time, the present world order has managed to place state concerns (including sovereignty and maintaining international peace and security) side by side with the principle of protecting and extending the dignity of individual human beings. This vision is not exclusively one of state power and a positive grant of rights by nations to people. Instead, it is at least partly premised on a natural law notion of the inherent worth of human beings, and is manifested in the elaboration of rules by which a state must treat its own citizens. Thus, the pendulum of natural and positive approaches to international legal obligation has swung back to a more neutral position in which the international community recognizes values separate and apart from state sovereignty. At the same time, the multi-faceted character of contemporary international relations has made international law relevant in more topical areas.

II. Sources of International Law

The sources of international legal obligation are unique, combining the use of materials and methods that are not often used in other legal systems in the United States. This section describes the primary sources for international law rules (general principles, custom, and international agreements such as treaties) and how decision-makers (including federal judges) have used these sources. U.S. courts have generally relied on Article 38 of the Statute of the International Court of Justice (ICJ Statute), which lists the sources of international law as:

(1) International conventions (i.e. treaties and other agreements), whether general or particular, establishing rules expressly recognized by consenting states;

(2) International custom, as evidence of a general practice accepted as law;

(3) The general principles of law recognized by civilized nations;

(4) Other sources and evidence of international law, such as judicial decisions and the teachings of the most highly qualified publicists of the various nations, as a subsidiary means for the determination of rules of law.

A. Treaties and Other International Agreements

1. General Features

a. Introduction International agreements, and in particular treaties, are an essential source of international law. Indeed, it is easy to think of written agreements between countries as being *the* source of international legal rules. The following section will focus on the international law of treaties and how it affects the legal obligations of states parties.

Although customary international law and general principles (discussed below) remain an important part of the dynamic of international law formation, treaties and treaty-making are gradually becoming the most frequently relied upon source of rules for international conduct. Because of this, the international community has adopted a number of instruments dealing with treaty formalities. The 1969 Vienna Convention on the Law of Treaties (VCLT) is the single-most definitive source on this subject, and even though the United States is not a party, it regards almost all of the VCLT's provisions as binding customary international law.[20] (The United States did originally criticize some of the VCLT's provisions on treaty interpretation and modification, but it is not clear whether it persists in these objections.) For the purpose of defining its own scope of application, Article 2 of the VCLT defines "treaty" as "an international agreement concluded between States in written form and governed by international law . . . whatever its particular designation." (The term

---

[20] For a history of the U.S. negotiation of the VCLT, see Richard D. Kearny & Robert E. Dalton, *The Treaty on Treaties*, 64 AM. J. INT'L L. 495 (1970).

"treaty" has a more particular meaning in U.S. constitutional law, which will be considered below at section III.B).

There are other types of international agreements in addition to treaties that are recognized as binding under international law, including agreements between a state and an international organization, and (on occasion) oral promises from one state to another. An international agreement may be designated by any number of terms, such as "treaty," "pact," "protocol," "convention," "covenant," or "declaration"; however, the title of an agreement does not normally in and of itself have any particular legal significance. Rather, for purposes of determining whether an agreement is potentially enforceable under international law, the intent of the parties to be legally bound, as expressed in the language of the agreement, is of crucial importance.

b. Bilateral and multilateral treaties As the respective terms suggest, *bilateral* treaties are those which are made between two nations, while *multilateral* treaties are those concluded among three or more countries. One of the legal effects of whether a treaty is bilateral or multilateral will be considered below in section II.A.3, discussing treaty breach. Moreover, the distinction between bilateral and multilateral treaties is sometimes important for purposes of locating treaty texts, whether in historical collections of treaties made before 1919 (like Parry's and Marten's), international collections (like the *League of Nations Treaty Series* (LNTS) or the *UN Treaty Series* (UNTS, now available online)), or national treaty sources (for the United States, *U.S. Treaties and Other International Agreements* (U.S.T.) or *Treaties and Other International Acts Series* (T.I.A.S.)).

c. Reservations A "reservation" is a statement by one treaty party, made during the process of signing, ratifying, or otherwise approving the treaty, which purports to change the legal effect of certain treaty provisions for that party.[21] Reservations normally arise in the context of multilateral treaties, where the potentially large number of parties that may sign the treaty—often over an extended period of time—complicates the treaty negotiation process and renders re-negotiation virtually impossible. Not all reservations are considered valid—for example, reservations cannot be incompatible with the object and purpose of the treaty. Moreover, other treaty parties have the right to object to reservations. The VCLT has provided rules for the acceptance of and objection to reservations for multilateral treaties,[22] but the result can be a patchwork quilt of different obligations among various parties to the same multilateral treaty. Reservations can thus complicate the question of what treaty obligations are in force for which treaty parties.

d. Default rules As for how treaties are applied and observed, it is worthwhile to keep in mind some basic default rules. First, international agreements are normally assumed to have only prospective effect. Retroactivity of treaty provisions is disfavored, so if the parties intend that a rule is to be applied to events occurring before the agreement is signed, they should so indicate.[23] Likewise, it is normally assumed that a treaty will be applied throughout the territorial

---

[21] *See* Vienna Convention on the Law of Treaties, 1155 U.N.T.S. 331, art. 2, para. 1(d) (*entered into force* Jan. 27, 1980) [hereinafter VCLT].
[22] *See* id. arts. 19, 20.
[23] *See* Galanis v. Pallanck, 568 F.2d 234 (2d Cir. 1977).

sovereignty of the state party. If for some reason a country does not wish a particular treaty-based rule to be applied to part of its territory, it would have to so provide or make the necessary reservation (assuming a reservation was permitted on that ground).

2. Treaty Interpretation

a. Basic Rules Aside from these issues of treaty application, the real difficulty in observance of international agreements arises from their interpretation.[24] Articles 31 and 32 of the VCLT sets forth the basic rules of treaty interpretation. The most fundamental rule is articulated in Article 31(1): "A treaty shall be interpreted in good faith in accordance with the ordinary meaning given to the terms of the treaty in their context and in the light of its object and purpose." Other provisions of Article 31 provide a specific definition of "context" and additional related guidance.

Types of evidence not referenced in Article 31—including the preparatory work of the treaty—are designated "supplementary means of interpretation" by Article 32. According to Article 32, such evidence may only be used in order to "confirm" the meaning that is suggested by an Article 31 analysis, or in circumstances where application of Article 31 leads to an ambiguous or manifestly absurd result.

b. Schools of Interpretation Notwithstanding the very specific hierarchy of relevant considerations laid out in Articles 31 and 32, there are discernable tendencies among different scholars—and even among

---

[24] *See, e.g.*, United States v. Stuart, 489 U.S. 353 (1989); Air France v. Saks, 470 U.S. 392 (1985); Factor v. Laubenheimer, 290 U.S. 276 (1933); The Amiable Isabella, 19 U.S. (6 Wheat.) 1 (1821).

different tribunals—to rely more heavily on one type of consideration than others in arriving at the final interpretation of a treaty provision. There are at least three commonly acknowledged "schools" or approaches to treaty interpretation, which correspond to methods for construction of any legal text—including constitutions, statutes, and contracts.

i. Textualist The first school is *textualism.* All solid treaty interpretation begins with the words of a provision itself, as they are commonly understood. VCLT Article 31, in discussing treaty interpretation, calls for an examination of a text's "ordinary meaning." Many treaties are drafted in two or more languages, and it is vital to ascertain not only which languages are "authentic," but also that there may be different shades of meanings of terms in different languages.[25]

ii. Intentionalist Textualism can be a form of contextual reading of different provisions in a treaty text, in order to reach a sensible result. Already one can see a tension between the text of a treaty provision and the intent of the drafters. However, the second, *intentionalist,* approach to treaty interpretation has never been popular in international law. Indeed, the VCLT relegates sources shedding light on the intent of the drafters—including the negotiating history (known as *travaux préparatoires,* or *travaux*) of a provision—to a secondary role.[26] They can be used only where the text is "ambiguous or obscure,"

---

[25] *See United States v. Percheman,* 32 U.S. (7 Pet.) 51 (1833), which reversed *Foster & Elam v. Neilson,* 27 U.S. (2 Pet.) 253 (1829), partially on the basis of a revised translation of a treaty text.

[26] *See* VCLT, *supra* note 21, art. 32.

or the plain meaning of the text leads to a "manifestly absurd or unreasonable" result.

One reason that *travaux* may be somewhat disfavored in international law is the concern that some countries might sign a treaty long after it was negotiated and signed. Should these newcomers be bound not only to the text, but also the informal understandings of the drafters? This would unduly privilege the interpretive positions of the original signatories. Likewise, use of negotiating history—including earlier drafts of a treaty, reports and commentaries, and diplomatic statements—can be selective and easily manipulated. Despite these cautions, use of *travaux* has become a constant feature of interpretive disputes over treaties, particularly as decided in U.S. courts.[27]

iii. Teleological That leaves the third school of interpretation: seeking to effectuate the purpose of a treaty, rather than slavishly following the text or attempting to divine the intent of the drafters. Known in international law as a *teleological* approach, it can also be called purposivism. It is captured in the VCLT's requirement that treaties be construed in light of their "object and purpose" and in view of "relevant rules of international law." The goal of this approach is to interpret a treaty in a way that gives scope to the fundamental reason or problem it was supposed to address. This approach is especially common with more "organic" or "constitutional" treaties, including those that establish international institutions (such as the United Nations Charter of 1945) or that fashion a "framework" for further international legislation. There are limits to teleology in treaty construction,

---

[27] *See* TWA v. Franklin Mint, 466 U.S. 243 (1984).

and interpreters cannot take the purpose of a treaty too far. For example, the ICJ has flatly rejected the notion of "maximum effectiveness"—construing a treaty so as to give it the fullest effect. In a 1950 Advisory Opinion,[28] the Court ruled that peace treaties concluded by eastern European states containing arbitration clauses could not be construed so as to give the UN Secretary General the power to appoint arbitrators, if the states themselves had refused to do so.

3. Suspension and Termination of Treaties

The most contentious issue in treaty law arises, however, when one state purports to unilaterally suspend or terminate an obligation in an international agreement. The debates over the withdrawal of the United States from the Anti-Ballistic Missile (ABM) Treaty and the "unsigning" of the International Criminal Court Statute are two recent examples. The VCLT and customary international law set forth situations in which a treaty may be terminated as well as situations that do not necessarily cause automatic termination.

a. Breach One situation in which a treaty may be terminated is when one party to a treaty believes that another state has failed to abide by the obligations of the agreement. International law clearly recognizes the right of a state to terminate a treaty if another party has breached its obligations under the agreement. Customary international law and VCLT Article 60 have added an important caveat: a nation cannot terminate the treaty unless another party has *materially* breached a provision "essential to the accomplishment of the

---

[28] Interpretation of Peace Treaties with Bulgaria, Hungary and Romania, 1950 I.C.J. 65, 221 (Mar. 30).

object or purpose of a treaty." In other words, a trivial breach of a treaty obligation does not give grounds for unilateral termination. Indeed, under this rule, if a party terminates a treaty because it believes the other side has committed a material breach, but later finds it was wrong in that belief, then *it* will be regarded as the party in breach. Of course, just because a state believes a treaty partner has committed a material breach does not necessarily mean, in practice, that termination will be forthcoming. It might just spark a renewed round of diplomacy in order to heal the rift.

This description contemplates a treaty relationship between two states (a bilateral treaty), but when there are multiple parties, a breach between two parties may change the status of the legal obligations as between those two parties, but the treaty would remain in force between all the parties who were not in dispute with one another.

b. Fundamental change Another ground for termination of treaties is known as the doctrine of fundamental change of circumstances, or *rebus sic stantibus*. Under this rule, a party may terminate, suspend or withdraw from a treaty when the conditions that led to the conclusion of a treaty change fundamentally in a manner not foreseen by the parties. Needless to say, such a doctrine has the potential of being utterly destructive of good faith and predictable observance of treaty obligations.[29] It has persisted in treaty law because of the need for a mechanism of peaceful alteration of treaty obligations when there are significant changes in material facts that gave rise to the treaty. Article 62 of the VCLT nonetheless

---

[29] *See* TWA v. Franklin Mint, *supra* note 27.

places strict limits on the circumstances in which *rebus sic stantibus* can be invoked; in practice, courts and tribunals have found these conditions to be met in very few cases.

c. Preserving obligations in cases of hostilities If international law has sought to limit terminations of international agreements because of changed circumstances, it has also sought to preserve treaty obligations threatened by an outbreak of hostilities between the parties. The termination of treaties by war has always been a matter of customary international law. In fact, it still is; the VCLT is deliberately silent on this subject. While there remains substantial controversy as to whether war cancels all treaty obligations, the better reasoned view is that an outbreak of hostilities only suspends those obligations the performance of which are incompatible with a state of conflict between the countries. For example, the New York Court of Appeals (Judge Cardozo writing) decided that a treaty provision giving rights of inheritance to foreigners was not affected by World War I.[30] Certain kinds of treaties—especially those prescribing humanitarian rules of war (like protecting civilians and prisoners of war)—are precisely those that are *not* terminated by war.

B. Customary International Law

1. Formation of Customary International Law

There are two key elements in the formation of a customary international law rule. They are elegantly and succinctly expressed in Article 38 of the ICJ Statute. Custom is "evidence of a general practice

---

[30] *See* Techt v. Hughes, 229 N.Y. 222 (1920).

accepted as law." To show a rule of customary international law, one must prove to the satisfaction of the relevant decision-maker (whether it be an international tribunal, domestic court, or government or inter-governmental actor) that the rule (1) has been followed as a "general practice," *and* (2) has been "accepted as law." Nonetheless, substantial difficulties face domestic courts when they are required to determine whether a particular norm qualifies as customary international law.[31]

a. General practice The first part of the equation (the general practice element) is an objective inquiry: have international actors really followed the rule? Has the practice been consistent? Has the practice been followed for a sufficient period of time?

b. Accepted as law The second part of the equation (the accepted-as-law element) has often been called a subjective, or even psychological, inquiry. It asks *why* an international actor has observed a particular practice. This is specifically known as *opinio juris sive necessitatus* (or just *opinio juris*), and it attempts to ascertain whether a practice is observed out of a sense of legal obligation or necessity, or, rather, merely out of courtesy, neighborliness, or expediency.

2. Discerning Whether Customary International Law Exists in a Particular Case

There is sometimes tension between these two elements. In trying to prove that something is a rule of customary international law, there is a tendency

---

[31] *See, e.g.*, Filartiga v. Peña-Irala, 630 F.2d 876 (2d Cir. 1980).

simply to document that a particular practice is really followed by states and other international actors and to forget about *why* the rule is observed. However, the *opinio juris* element is equally important; otherwise, international actors will be bound to follow practices that may not reflect their own expectations of lawful or obligatory international conduct. It would, for example, be easy to document a common practice among states of sending their heads of state to attend the funeral services of another head of state, but it would surely be wrong to conclude that they are therefore under a legal obligation to do so in the future.

There also is no requirement that a practice necessarily be observed for a long period of time before it will be confirmed as a binding custom. The history of international law is replete with examples of state practice that enjoyed such immediate popularity, and around which formed such a complete consensus of the international community, that they were recognized almost as "instant custom." One well-known example was the development of state claims to offshore oil and gas deposits under a theory of continental shelves that took barely 15 years to form into binding law. It is not the age of a practice that makes a custom. Rather, it is the high degree of consistency and uniformity of observance by most (if not all) of the international community that satisfies the objective element of confirming it as a "general practice."

One of the best examples of the hard work of lawyering evidence of state practice is shown in *The Paquete Habana*, a case decided by the U.S. Supreme Court in 1900.[32] The facts and issues presented in

---

[32] 175 U.S. 677 (1900). For other prominent examples of federal courts applying customary international law, see *De Sanchez v. Banco Central de Nicaragua*, 770 F.2d 1385, 1397

the case were deceptively simple. Two Cuban fishing boats had been captured by U.S. naval forces in the Spanish-American War and condemned as "prizes" of war. The question was whether small coastal fishing boats were immune from capture under customary international law. Drawing from sources as varied as medieval English royal ordinances, agreements between European nations, orders issued to the U.S. Navy in earlier conflicts, and the opinions of treatise writers, the Supreme Court held that custom barred the capture of small fishing boats.

The boat owner's victory was not only a demonstration of an eclectic and scholarly collection of evidence of state practice; it was a *tour de force* of powerful argument insofar as it persuaded a majority of the Justices that the immunity granted to coastal fishing boats was grounded in humanitarian concerns as well as supported by legal obligation. The United States had particularly relied on one earlier case, *The Young Jacob*, decided by the English High Court of Admiralty in 1798.[33] That case had held that the practice of immunizing fishing craft was not a rule at all, but instead was only "comity" or courtesy. The English court had ruled that the practice was not supported by *opinio juris*, and the United States (a century later) seized on this as a basis for arguing that protecting enemy fishing boats was a matter of "grace" only. The boat owners persuaded the Court, however, that within the intervening century the

---

(5th Cir. 1985) and *Forti v. Suarez-Mason*, 694 F. Supp. 707, 710–11 (N.D. Cal. 1988). *See also* RESTATEMENT, *supra* note 2, § 113, cmt. b, "Judicial notice of international law" (stating "The determination of international law or the interpretation of an agreement is a question of law for the court, not a question of fact for a jury.").

[33] 1 C. Rob. 20, 165 Eng. Rep. 81 (Adm. 1798) (Eng.).

practice *had* become obligatory; it was no longer optional and was, indeed, binding on the United States.

3. Opting out of a Customary Norm

It is important to emphasize that states may opt out of the development of a custom by persistently objecting to the emerging norm. Objections can take the form of diplomatic demarches or concrete action that reflects opposition to the rule. There are, however, some rules of custom that are so significant that the international community will not suffer states to dissent from being bound or to "contract" out of them by treaty. For example, two states may not conclude a treaty reciprocally granting themselves the right to commit genocide against a selected group. These peremptory rules are called *jus cogens* norms.[34] Likewise, some customary international law obligations are so significant that the international community will permit *any* state to bring a claim for their violation, not just the countries immediately affected. These are *erga omnes* norms.

4. Conflicts Between a Treaty and Customary International Law

At times, one may find that a treaty does not agree with a customary norm and a question of priority arises. According to the *Restatement*,

> A subsequent agreement will prevail over prior custom, except where the principle of customary law has the character of *jus cogens,* but an agreement is ordinarily presumed to supplement rather than replace a customary rule. Provisions

---

[34] *See* RESTATEMENT, *supra* note 2, § 102, Reporters' Note 6, "Peremptory norms."

in international agreements are superseded by principles of customary international law that develop subsequently, where the parties to the agreement so intend, in which case the earlier provision in the agreement is deemed to have expired by mutual agreement or by desuetude. If an international agreement provides for denunciation, it will ordinarily be assumed that the agreement was not intended to be replaced by subsequent custom unless the parties denounce the earlier agreement.[35]

However, as noted in section III.A.4, below, the most widely accepted view under U.S. law is that a customary international law rule cannot take precedence over a pre-existing contrary statute or treaty.

C. General Principles of Law

1. Effects of Domestic Law on International Law

As used in Article 38 of the ICJ Statute "general principles of law" refers to principles of domestic law (sometimes called "municipal law"), as recognized in the legal systems of "civilized nations." The process by which a principle is "elevated" from various domestic legal systems to the realm of international law is subtle and complex. The very language of Article 38 is suggestive that a principle would have to be "recognized" not just in one legal system, but rather, in most of the world's legal cultures. The reference in Article 38 to "civilized nations" is generally construed as referring to jurisdictions embracing the common law tradition (the United Kingdom and its

---

[35] *See* RESTATEMENT, *supra* note 2, § 102, Reporters' Note 4, "Conflict between customary law and international agreement" (citation omitted); *see also* VCLT, *supra* note 21.

former colonies, as well as the United States), the civil law derived from ancient Roman law (prevalent in all of continental Europe, Latin America, and most of Africa and Asia), significant religious legal cultures (including Islamic law), and ideological legal systems (including socialist law as practiced in China and elsewhere).

There is a bit of a paradox in the incorporation of general principles as international legal rules. The more abstract the principle, the greater consensus of legal systems, but also the less useful the rule. Some general principles of this sort include a rule of good faith in international obligations (known as *pacta sunt servanda*) and the doctrines of necessity and self-defense. These are useful doctrines, but they are short on specifics. On the other hand, the less abstract (and more concrete) the principle, the more useful it is, but also the more difficult it is to find a consensus among domestic legal systems.

A good example of this paradox at work is the rather prosaic principle that there should be a period of repose (i.e. a statute of limitations) for international claims. Almost all domestic legal systems have a similar principle. In 1903, an international arbitral tribunal ruled that there was sufficient consensus to make it a rule of international claims practice (and thus to bar a nearly 30-year-old claim). But the tribunal could not say definitively whether the international statute of limitations was 10 years, 30 years, or 50 years.[36] The abstract principle of prescription was thus recognized, but no specific rule or time limit.

---

[36] Gentini (Italy) Claim (Venezuelan Mixed Cl. Comm'n 1903), *in* JACKSON RALSTON, VENEZUELAN ARBITRATIONS OF 1903, at 720 (1904).

2. U.S. Practice

While it is rare for U.S. judges to confront international law cases in which general principles are implicated, it does periodically occur.[37] In such matters, U.S. courts are obliged to canvass a wide spectrum of domestic legal systems in order to ascertain whether a principle has risen to the level of an international law rule. At the same time, international tribunals have relied on U.S. jurisprudence to establish general principles. One example is the establishment of basic rules of international environmental law (discussed further at section IV.D.2 below).

D. Other Sources and Evidence of International Law

Court decisions, legislation of international bodies, and equitable principles do not have the legal significance in international law that they have in U.S. law. They are recognized in ICJ Statute Article 38, but only as a subsidiary means of establishing *evidence* of the content of international law norms. By contrast, Article 38 gives more weight to the scholarly writings of "highly qualified publicists" than that normally afforded by U.S. courts.

1. Case Law of Courts and Tribunals

"Judicial decisions" are one of two specific "other sources" specifically mentioned in Article 38 as a "subsidiary" means of determining the content of

---

[37] *See* United States v. Cadena, 585 F.2d 1252, 1264 (9th Cir. 1975); United States v. MacAllister, 160 F.3d 1304, 1308–09 (D.C. Cir. 1984); Beanal v. Freeport McMoran, *Inc.*, 969 F. Supp. 362, 384 (E.D. La. 1997), aff'd, 197 F.3d 161 (5th Cir. 1999).

international law norms. As noted in the Introduction, there is a wide body of case law from international courts and tribunals that can be examined—not to mention the decisions of domestic courts on international matters, including the identification of general principles of law accepted by civilized nations. In this sense, while international tribunals do not normally follow the principle of *stare decisis,* previous judicial decisions can nonetheless play a significant—albeit "subsidiary"—role in developing the substance of international law.

2. Teachings of Highly Qualified Publicists

The ICJ Statute specifically recognizes the "teachings of the most highly qualified publicists of the various nations" as evidence of rules of law. In short, the writings of international law academics and practitioners—"publicists" in the language of the Statute—can constitute evidence of international law. The U.S. Supreme Court, as early as 1820, indicated that "the law of nations... may be ascertained by consulting the works of jurists, writing professionally on public law...." United States v. Smith, 18 U.S. (5 Wheat.) 153, 160–61 (1820). "Such works are resorted to by judicial tribunals, not for the speculations of their authors concerning what the law ought to be, but for trustworthy evidence of what the law really is." The Paquete Habana, 175 U.S. at 699 (*citing* Ware v. Hylton, 3 U.S. (3 Dall.) 199, 226–27 (1796)).

3. Equitable Principles

Equity is often mentioned as a subsidiary source of international law. To be sure, equity and fairness is a general principle of law recognized by all civilized legal systems, and would be incorporated into international law by that avenue. Many equitable principles have been vigorously employed in international dispute settlement. One such concept is "abuse of right," where an international actor is recognized as having the freedom to engage in certain conduct, but is barred from pursuing a course of action in certain circumstances or in a particular fashion.[38] Likewise, "unjust enrichment" has been used by international tribunals to give relief to an actor disadvantaged by a transaction, even though no formal contractual relationship existed. Finally, the World Court has invoked the doctrine of "clean hands"—a party that seeks equity must do equity. Thus, in the *Diversion of Water from the River Meuse*,[39] the PCIJ rejected mutual claims by The Netherlands and Belgium that each had impermissibly altered the flow of their boundary waters as each had altered the flow of the river.

There are two important caveats to the application of equitable or fairness doctrines in international law. The first is that equity does not mean reaching a result that is regarded as balanced—i.e., a judicial compromise. Such an outcome is the province of negotiation and mediation and is not regarded as being a legitimate application of a legal approach to dispute settlement. In recognition of this, Article 38 of the ICJ Statute expressly bars the Court from deciding cases *ex aequo et bono* ("what is just and good") unless the parties expressly agree to that. Similarly, equity does not mean equality. Despite strong efforts to fashion international law doctrines to serve the ends of distributional and social justice, international tribunals are not supposed to place judicial fingers on the scales in this fashion.

---

[38] *See* Cayuga Indians (Gr. Brit. v. U.S.), 6 U.N. Rep. Int'l Arb. Awards 173 (U.S.-Brit. Arb. Trib. 1926).
[39] (Neth. v. Belg.) 1937 P.C.I.J. (ser. A/B) No. 70 (June 28).

4. The Role of General Assembly Resolutions

There is no central legislature in international law, no World Parliament. (The specific role of the United Nations will be discussed at section IV.B.) While there is a growing network of international institutions producing a body of international regulatory schemes, these are all in the form of treaty regimes. Suggestions, therefore, that the resolutions of UN bodies (particularly the General Assembly, where each nation has one vote) constitute a binding source of international law are extravagant. These intimations have been properly construed as an attempt to provide an easy way to make international law rules, apart from custom and treaty and without states' consent to be bound. This is not to say, though, that the UN is powerless to make binding rules for its own operations. The question, instead, is whether General Assembly resolutions, which are only "recommendations" under Article 10 of the UN Charter, can make law.

One point that has often been made by commentators is that General Assembly resolutions, precisely because they are recommendations, lack the necessary *opinio juris* for custom.[40] This is so even though states may repeatedly vote for a resolution and profess their support for the legal rule it stands for. States, for example, overwhelmingly voted in the General Assembly for resolutions condemning state-sponsored torture, yet (as such groups as Amnesty International have reported) some of these same states actually engage in the torture of their own citizens. Which do we prefer to believe: the professed position of the state, or the empirical evidence of its actual conduct?

---

[40] *See* RESTATEMENT, *supra* note 2, § 103, Reporters' Note 2, "Declaratory resolutions of international organizations."

In some instances, international lawyers and judges will take states' words at face value. For example, a U.S. court decided that torture constituted a violation of the "law of nations" for purposes of invoking the court's jurisdiction under the Alien Tort Claims Act.[41] In reaching that conclusion, the Second Circuit of the U.S. Court of Appeals relied on General Assembly resolutions while properly noting that they constituted evidence only (but persuasive evidence) of state practice and *opinio juris*. The votes themselves, the court was careful to say, were not dispositive as a source of international legal obligation.[42]

---

[41] 28 U.S.C. § 1350 (2003).
[42] Filartiga v. Peña-Irala, 630 F.2d 876 (2d Cir. 1980).

III. PUBLIC INTERNATIONAL LAW AND U.S. LAW

International law both influences and has independent status in domestic legal systems, and (conversely) domestic law affects international law. International law is not usually incorporated into domestic law automatically, and the United States is no exception in this regard. This process of incorporation is an aspect of the United States' "law of foreign relations," and it regulates the way that public international law becomes part of U.S. law (both state and federal). This section examines how international law rules interact with U.S. constitutional law and statutory and common law sources of law. Additionally, the precise way that the United States' obligations in international agreements are enforced in U.S. courts will be examined.

A. The Interrelationship of International Law and Domestic Law

1. Introduction: Monism and Dualism

International law is substantially influenced by domestic law. That can be seen by the reference to general principles of national law "recognized by civilized nations" as a source of international legal obligation. Precise rules of domestic law may be interpreted and applied by international tribunals in disputes between states. In other words, the relationship between international law and domestic law is a "two-way street." International law's use of domestic law, however, is constrained by a number of important principles.

International law assumes that its obligations will be implemented through domestic law and legal institutions. But the international legal system is indifferent as to *how* international legal obligations are carried out by a particular state, provided they are effectively implemented. Two distinct traditions have developed with respect to the incorporation of international law into domestic law, and scholars continue to debate the merits of each. The *monist* approach, in essence, is based on the idea that international law and domestic law are parts of the same legal system, but that international law is higher in prescriptive value than national law. A *dualist* approach, by contrast, assumes that international law and domestic law are separate and distinct legal systems that operate on different levels, and that international law can only be enforced in national law if it is incorporated or transformed. The United States can rightly be regarded as a dualist nation, as reflected in the answers to the following inquiries.

2. International Law and the Constitution

a. Domestic effects of international law The first and most important inquiry in examining the U.S. legal system is whether international law can prevail over the Constitution. The answer is an emphatic "no," and for this reason alone the United States qualifies as a dualist nation. The U.S. Constitution is certainly not silent on matters of international law and foreign relations. Treaty-making powers are allocated, and the effect of international agreements is provided for. Congress is even granted the power to "define and punish offenses against the law of nations," just as it is permitted to legislate on matters of foreign commerce.[43] The President is given the authority to receive and send ambassadors, as well as being commander-in-chief of the armed forces, even though Congress is given the power to "declare war." Lastly, the federal judiciary is seemingly given the authority to resolve disputes involving international questions, and is explicitly granted jurisdiction over admiralty and maritime disputes, as well as those involving foreign ambassadors.

It is now well-established in U.S. law that neither a rule of customary international law nor a provision of a treaty can abrogate a right granted under the Constitution. In the leading case, *Reid v. Covert*,[44] the U.S. Supreme Court made in 1957 a ruling concerning an executive agreement governing the status of U.S. armed forces and their dependents stationed in occupied Germany after World War II. The agreement provided that the dependents of army personnel were subject to court martial for any crimes committed in Germany. A plurality of the Supreme Court held that the fact that a court martial was permissible under the treaty did not abrogate the defendants' Sixth Amendment right to a regular jury trial by their peers.

b. International obligation The fact that the U.S. Supreme Court might rule that a treaty obligation or rule of custom is unconstitutional does *not* necessarily mean that the United States would be relieved of its international obligations to fulfill that treaty or custom. In these circumstances, the United States' *international* obligations will persist until the custom is changed or the treaty is terminated; they will not,

---

[43] U.S. CONST, art. I, § 8.
[44] 354 U.S. 1 (1957).

however, have any domestic effect. This means the United States has responsibility to other countries for any breach of the international rule, even if no U.S. court would enforce the obligation. That is a key aspect of practicing international law in a dualist jurisdiction: a particular obligation may be binding on the state in its international relations, and yet have no force in its internal law.

3. The Role of Customary International Law

The second inquiry relevant to the monist/dualist question is whether customary international law is part of federal common law or state common law. As posited, this question only concerns the status of customary international law in U.S. law. Under the Supremacy Clause of Article VI of the Constitution, treaties are unambiguously regarded as part of federal law. Because the Supremacy Clause does not mention customary international law, doubts continually have been raised as to whether custom is part of federal law or the law of the individual states of the Union. This may not appear to be significant until one recalls that if an issue is a matter of state law, federal courts should apply that state law, and not a supposed federal general common law.[45] Moreover, whether customary international law is state law may also affect the jurisdiction of federal courts in hearing such matters.

The view of most courts and commentators is that customary international law is federal law. This means, at a minimum, that cases involving claims to exclusively customary international law rights and duties (some kinds of diplomatic immunities or law

---

[45] This is the rule of *Erie R.R. Co. v. Tompkins*, 304 U.S. 64 (1938).

of the sea privileges, for example) may be decided by the federal courts.[46] Whether this conclusion also extends a grant to the federal courts of a power to make a judge-made federal common law of foreign relations is more controversial, and will have to be settled by future litigation.

4. Customary International Law and Federalism

The third important question regarding the role of international law in the U.S. legal system is whether states of the Union are obliged to observe customary international law. Again, this problem arises from the fact that the Constitution's Supremacy Clause does not specifically mention customary international law as a source of law that preempts contrary state law. An analytically distinct question is whether there exists a dormant foreign relations power granted to the federal government that prevents the states from legislating (even in the absence of Congressional action) in a manner contrary to the foreign relations interests of the country. The U.S. Supreme Court has intimated such, ruling that an Oregon statute discriminating against certain foreigners in inheritance matters had a direct impact on foreign relations and was preempted even in the absence of a conflicting federal statute.[47] This matter is intensely controversial, although there have been a number of recent Supreme Court decisions that

---

[46] RESTATEMENT, *supra* note 2, § 111 (1), (2). *But see* Bergman v. De Sieyes, 170 F.2d 360 (2d Cir. 1948).
[47] *See* Zschernig v. Miller, 389 U.S. 429 (1968); *see also* Amer. Ins. Assoc. v. Garamendi, 539 U.S. ___; 123 S.Ct. 2374 (2003) (applying *Zschernig* and discussing the "contrasting theories of field and conflict pre-emption evident in the *Zschernig* opinions").

have struck down state statutes as being preempted by acts of Congress.[48]

5. Customary International Law and Federal Statutes

A final relevant inquiry is whether customary international law can be "trumped" by federal statutes and executive determinations. This implicates the precise status of customary international law in relation to other sources of *federal* law. The most widely accepted view, although it has not been authoritatively determined, is that customary international law rules cannot take precedence over a pre-existing contrary statute (or treaty), at least in U.S. domestic law.[49] Nevertheless, treaties or statutes should be interpreted and applied in view of more recent developments in custom. Moreover, an old rule contained in a statute or international agreement could well be changed by a new law or treaty that codifies a later change in custom. But where there is no statute or treaty on point, U.S. courts are obliged to follow rules of customary international law. Justice Gray ably made this point in 1900 in *The Paquete Habana* case, when he observed:

> International law is part of our law, and must be ascertained and administered by the courts of

---

[48] *See* United States v. Locke, 120 S. Ct. 1135 (2000); Crosby v. National Foreign Trade Council, 120 S. Ct. 2288 (2000). *But see* Barclays Bank PLC v. Franchise Tax Bd. of Cal., 512 U.S. 298 (1994).

[49] *See* RESTATEMENT, *supra* note 2, § 115, Comment d Reporters' Note 4, "Rule of international law inconsistent with pre-existing United States law or agreement"; *compare with* §102 Reporter's Note 4, "Sources of International law."

justice of appropriate jurisdiction as often as questions of right depending upon it are duly presented for their determination. For this purpose, where there is no treaty and no controlling executive or legislative act or judicial decision, resort must be had to the customs and usages of civilized nations. . . .[50]

A related question is whether the president has the legal authority to violate customary international law. Court decisions are mixed on this point.[51] A number of decisions indicate that the president or senior officers of the executive branch are not prohibited from taking actions in violation of customary international law, and courts will often extend substantial deference to executive branch positions as to the content of that law. Such deference may depend on whether the authority being exercised by the executive branch falls within the president's exclusive powers under Article II of the Constitution. In some cases, courts may decline to rule on the merits of cases involving customary international law for fear of answering a "political question,"[52] although the Supreme Court has indicated that foreign relations issues are not wholly beyond the competence of the courts.[53]

---

[50] 175 U.S. 677, 700 (1900).
[51] Compare *Garcia-Mir v. Meese*, 788 F.2d 1446 (11th Cir. 1986) and Gisbert v. United States Attorney-General, 988 F.2d 1437 (5th Cir. 1993) with *Fernandez v. Wilkinson*, 505 F. Supp. 787 (D. Kan. 1980), *aff'd on other grounds*, 654 F.2d 1382 (10th Cir. 1981).
[52] *See* Made in the USA Found. v. United States, 242 F.3d 1300 (11th Cir. 2001).
[53] *See* Japan Whaling Ass'n v. Amer. Cetacean Soc'y, 478 U.S. 221 (1986).

B. Treaties and the Laws of the United States

1. The Treaty Power

a. Constitutional provisions The Constitution has two clauses concerning treaties. Article II, Section 2 provides that the president "shall have the Power, by and with the Advice and Consent of the Senate, to make Treaties, provided two-thirds of the Senators present concur." Article VI, Section 2—the Supremacy Clause—provides:

> This Constitution, and the Laws of the United States which shall be made in Pursuance thereof; and all Treaties made, or which shall be made, under the Authority of the United States, shall be the supreme Law of the Land; and the Judges in every State shall be bound thereby, any Thing in the Constitution or Laws of any State to the Contrary notwithstanding.

These two clauses together establish the mechanism for treaties to be adopted and their consequent effect as law. Even so, many questions remain about the nature and limits of the treaty power.

b. "Advice and Consent" and RUDs A few points of clarification need to be made. In popular parlance, the Senate "ratifies" treaties that are presented by the president. That is a misnomer; the Senate actually "advises and consents" to a treaty (according to the actual language of the Constitution). The President then has the discretion to later "proclaim" the treaty and conclude the ratification process. In recent years, the Senate has often conditioned its advice and consent on the attachment of various reservations, understandings, and declarations (RUDs) to the treaty. Although only reservations purport to change the legal effect of a treaty, Senatorial understandings and interpretations may also be regarded as contentious and unwelcome by the executive branch. There have been occasional legal disputes about the permissible scope of certain reservations, and while the courts have validated many RUDs,[54] at least one court has ruled that the Senate may not condition its advice and consent on a reservation that has nothing to do with the international legal obligations contained in the treaty.[55]

c. Constitutional limitations on the Treaty Power

There have been efforts throughout U.S. history to restrain or cabin the treaty power. The perceived need for such restraint may derive from a sense that a source of law that is made exclusively by the president and the upper chamber of Congress (the Senate) is somehow undemocratic, in that it excludes the House of Representatives from the process. Constitutional limitations on the treaty power are found in the Bill of Rights and in the Constitution's federal structure.

i. The Bill of Rights One recognized limit on the treaty power is that treaties may not abrogate an individual liberty granted under the first eight amendments in the Bill of Rights. That follows from the ruling in the *Reid v. Covert* decision, which is the closest the Supreme Court has ever come to ruling an international agreement unconstitutional.

ii. Federalism Other limits on the treaty power have been poorly understood and even after centuries of speculation remain controversial. One such

---

[54] *See* Beazley v. Johnson, 242 F.3d 248 (5th Cir. 2001); Igartua de la Rosa v. United States, 32 F.3d 8 (1st Cir. 1994).
[55] *See* Power Auth. of N.Y. v. Fed. Power Comm'n, 247 F2d 538 (D.C. Cir. 1957).

potential limitation is federalism, the proper allocation of power between the national and state governments. The key question raised by federalism concerns is whether the Constitution's structural clauses reserve a field of authority to the states such that the federal government cannot legislate either by statute or treaty. The leading case on this subject remains the Supreme Court's 1920 decision in *Missouri v. Holland*.[56]

In a short opinion by Justice Holmes, the Court ruled in favor of the federal interest and held that the Migratory Bird Treaty (MBT) did not violate any federalism limits on the treaty power, even though Congress's power to enact legislation concerning migratory birds under the Commerce Clause had earlier been challenged. He observed that "it is obvious that there may be matters of the sharpest exigency for the national well being that an act of Congress could not deal with but that a treaty followed by such an act could." Because "the treaty in question does not contravene any prohibitory words to be found in the Constitution," the Court ruled that it was not barred by the Tenth Amendment or other federalism clauses. Holmes ruled that if a treaty was (1) necessitated by exigency and great national interests and (2) did not violate an express constitutional prohibition, then it could grant to Congress law-making authority it did not otherwise have under Article I of the Constitution.

There was one attempt to override the *Missouri v. Holland* decision by constitutional amendment in the 1950s. The proposed Bricker Amendment said that "a treaty shall become effective as internal law in the United States through legislation that would be valid in the absence of a treaty." The amendment

---

[56] 252 U.S. 416 (1920).

was narrowly defeated in Congress. The issue of federalism restraints on the treaty power receded over time, particularly as the Supreme Court consistently ruled that virtually every form of legislation was permitted under the Commerce Clause of Article I. Although there was speculation that a treaty could not legislate in a "forbidden zone" of authority granted to the states (such as state boundaries or state militias), this was never tested. Now that the Supreme Court has come to impose new limits on Congress's power under the Commerce Clause—and has struck down some statutes as violating those limits—the issue raised in *Missouri v. Holland* may return to the fore.

iii. Rejected theories of limitation Other suggested grounds for limiting the treaty power have posed fewer difficulties. The idea that treaties are limited in subject matter to topics of "international concern," although mooted by Chief Justice Charles Evans Hughes in remarks before the American Society of International Law in 1929,[57] is one that has only rarely been alluded to by courts,[58] and may be judicially unenforceable (given the blurring of international and domestic issues). Under such a theory, the United States could have some difficulty concluding agreements such as human rights treaties, which affect the rights that the United States affords its own citizens.

Another proffered, but ultimately rejected, limitation on the treaty power arises from the fact that treaties that require later legislative action on the part of the United States may not have immediate effect, to the extent that such action requires a vote by the House of Representatives. For example, a treaty

---

[57] *See* 23 AM. SOC'Y INT'L L. PROC. 194 (1929).
[58] *But see* Geofroy v. Riggs, 133 U.S. 258, 267 (1890).

that constituted a declaration of war would be unconstitutional, since the House must vote on such a declaration. Likewise, no treaty may automatically be regarded as authorization to spend moneys, since that too requires House action. However, a contention that the 1977 Panama Canal Treaty was unconstitutional because it violated the House of Representatives's right to vote on dispositions of U.S. property was rejected,[59] since the Property Clause (like most other constitutional provisions) does not vest the House of Representatives with specific decision-making authority.

2. Judicial Enforcement of Treaties

The question of whether and how treaties may be enforced in U.S. courts as part of the "law of the land" under the Supremacy Clause of the Constitution raises a number of challenging issues, including (1) the distinction between self-executing and non–self-executing treaties, (2) the operation of the "last-in-time" rule when a statute contradicts a treaty, and (3) concerns arising from the termination of treaties. Each of these will be reviewed in turn.

a. Self-executing and non–self-executing treaties

i. The question of self-execution of a treaty

Although the Supremacy Clause does not appear to contemplate a distinction between treaties to be given automatic force in U.S. domestic law and those that are not, just such a differentiation was made soon after the founding of the Republic. The 1829 case of *Foster & Elam v. Neilson*[60] concerned the application

---

[59] *See* Edwards v. Carter, 580 F.2d 1055 (D.C. Cir. 1978).
[60] 27 U.S. (2 Pet.) 253 (1829), *partially overruled by* United States v. Percheman, 32 U.S. (7 Pet.) 51 (1833).

of an 1819 treaty with Spain that (among other provisions) transferred sovereignty over Florida to the United States. The question presented was whether the treaty acted to confirm a land grant previously made by the Spanish crown. The Supreme Court concluded that the treaty had no such direct effect on the property rights of private claimants. Writing for the Court, Chief Justice John Marshall introduced into U.S. law a distinction between treaties that were to have immediate application without the necessity of implementing legislation by Congress *(self-executing* treaties) and those agreements that needed a subsequent act in order to have binding effect domestically (*non–self-executing* treaties). The Court concluded that while the rest of the 1819 treaty was self-executing, Article 8 required additional implementing legislation.

Some clauses in a treaty may be regarded as self-executing, while others are not. Some rules followed by federal courts are that if implementation of a treaty provision requires further legislative action, then it is non–self-executing; that provision will likely not be judicially enforceable unless a subsequent act of Congress makes it so. This is especially true if the contemplated subsequent action involves an issue over which the House of Representatives is clearly given a legislative role (such as making an appropriation of money or declaring war). Another rule is that treaties that provide that "certain acts shall not be done, or that certain limitations or restrictions shall not be disregarded or exceeded" by the parties, will be regarded as self-executing.[61] Another guide is whether the treaty provision is specific enough in content and manifests an intent by the parties to be binding in U.S. law (and enforceable by U.S. courts)

---

[61] Commonwealth v. Hawes, 76 Ky. (13 Bush) 697, 702–03 (1878).

without further implementing legislation. If so, it is self-executing; if not, it is non–self-executing.

ii. Private rights of action Problems of self-execution are particularly acute when the issue is whether an individual can directly claim a right under a treaty. Although this may be an analytically distinct question from self-execution, the two are often conflated. In large measure, this problem reflects a growing trend that treaties are intended not only to adjust relations between nations, but also to facilitate commerce, promote human rights, protect the environment, and allow for greater individual contacts between nations. U.S. courts have tended to find no "private right of action" under a treaty where the agreement is too vague (such as the UN Charter's human rights provisions[62]) or simply does not provide for such a right (like the peace treaties concluded with Germany after World War II[63]). In a similar way, courts have ruled that many of the critical conventions for the law of the sea and the laws of war are not judicially enforceable. At the same time, courts have generally held that extradition treaties and key private international law instruments (including the 1929 Warsaw Convention on airline liability and various Hague Conventions on international civil procedure) are self-executing and give rise to private rights of action.

iii. Application In the vast majority of these cases, judges use methods of treaty interpretation to decide the combined questions of self-execution and

---

[62] *See* Sei Fujii v. California, 38 Cal. 2d 718, 724, 242 P.2d 617, 621–22 (1952).

[63] *See* Dreyfus v. Von Finck, 534 F.2d 24 (2d Cir. 1976); Iwanowa v. Ford Motor Co., 67 F. Supp. 2d 424 (D.N.J. 1999).

private right of action. One court looked at a number of factors: the object and purpose of the treaty provision, the existence of alternative domestic procedures for implementation and enforcement, and whether our treaty partners recognize the private right of action.[64] In a growing trend, the administration that proposes a treaty (and the Senate that advises and consents to it) will explicitly state whether the treaty is to be regarded as self-executing. Such a statement is at least one promising piece of evidence for lawyers and courts to consider in making this determination.

If it is decided that a treaty provision is non-self-executing, many problems of the judicial role in treaty implementation are resolved. The parties will have to look to subsequent implementing legislation by Congress or perhaps to implementing actions by the executive branch. If there is no such implementing measure, the treaty is not judicially enforceable. If there is such a measure, then the implementing statute or regulation will be applied and interpreted, as consistently with the original treaty as is possible. If a treaty provision is found to be self-executing, however, the question of private rights of action may still need to be addressed before determining to what extent, if any, the provision may be judicially enforceable in U.S. courts.

b. The Last-in-Time Rule

i. Later Treaty/Earlier Statute Where a later treaty conflicts with an earlier statute, which prevails (for purposes of domestic application through the courts) depends on the issue of self-execution.[65] If

---

[64] *See* United States v. Postal, 589 F.2d 862 (5th Cir. 1979).
[65] *See* Whitney v. Robertson, 124 U.S. 190 (1888).

the later treaty is self-executing, then the earlier statute is considered abrogated to the extent it actually conflicts with the new international agreement. This is known as the "last-in-time" rule.[66] However, if the new treaty is non–self-executing, then it has no domestic force, and does not pose a domestic law conflict, until such time as Congress elects to implement the treaty through domestic legislation. (And, of course, a later statute always trumps a contrary, earlier act.)

ii. Later Statute/Earlier Treaty A similar question is raised when a later statute conflicts with an earlier international agreement of the United States. In this case, the treaty continues to have force on the international plane (until terminated on its own terms or in accordance with the law of treaties) but may not be enforceable by domestic courts or administrative authorities. Here, the assumption is that Congress is free to override or abrogate the domestic effect of the United States' treaty obligations.[67] Of course, such action has no effect on the United States' international duties.

iii. Qualifications to application of the rule
There are, however, some qualifications to this application of the last-in-time principle. The first is narrow and technical: A later statute that abrogates an earlier treaty cannot eliminate any rights that had vested under that agreement. The second consideration is more important—the notion that "an Act of Congress ought never to be construed to violate the law of nations if any other possible construction" is

---

[66] *See, e.g.*, The Head Money Cases, 112 U.S. 580 (1884); Diggs v. Shultz, 470 F.2d 461 (D.C. Cir. 1972), *cert. denied*, 411 U.S. 931 (1973).

[67] *See* Chae Chan Ping v. United States, 130 U.S. 581 (1889).

possible. This is known as the canon of the *Charming Betsy* case,[68] and it remains a significant principle of statutory construction to this day. It means, at a minimum, that a statute will not be allowed to abrogate the domestic enforcement of an earlier treaty (or rule of custom, for that matter) unless the Congressional intent to override that obligation is clear and manifest. This is obviously intended as an antidote to possible legislative inadvertence, but it also implicitly demands a high level of political resolve from Congress to enact bills in conflict with international law. Periodically, the *Charming Betsy* rule has saved the United States from profound diplomatic embarrassment, as with the attempted shutdown in 1987 of the UN observer mission of the Palestine Liberation Organization (PLO).[69]

c. Treaty termination issues The last point to be considered about the binding legal effect of treaties is what happens when an agreement is purportedly terminated. Termination of a treaty is a decision that is firmly committed to the political branches of the U.S. government. Private parties may not argue before a court that a treaty cannot be applied because our treaty partners have breached it.[70] Until the political branches take action to terminate or suspend an agreement, U.S. courts are obliged to give that agreement domestic effect as part of the "law of the land."

However, one separation-of-powers aspect of treaty termination remains a contentious—and unresolved—issue. It has been presumed that the president, acting alone, can initiate the needed action to

---

[68] 6 U.S. (2 Cranch) 64, 118 (1804).
[69] *See* United States v. Palestine Liberation Org., 695 F. Supp. 1456 (S.D.N.Y. 1988).
[70] *See* Charlton v. Kelly, 229 U.S. 447 (1913).

end the United States' treaty obligations under international law, and thus can end an agreement's domestic effect as well. Some have suggested that if it requires the president and the Senate acting together to *enter into* a treaty, then surely the same combination is required for action to *end* the agreement. Although this issue has reached the Supreme Court at least once—with President Carter's unilateral termination of a Mutual Defense Treaty with Taiwan in 1979—it still remains unsettled because a plurality of the Court declined to decide this issue on "political question" grounds.[71]

3. Executive Agreements

Treaties are not the exclusive means by which the United States can enter into legally binding arrangements with other nations under international law. In fact, the number of treaties submitted to the Senate for advice and consent has dwindled, while alternative forms of agreement (called executive agreements) have flourished. As of January 2003, the United States had concluded less than 1000 treaties, while it had entered into more than 15,000 executive agreements. In terms of sheer volume, executive agreements have assumed a degree of substantial importance.

There are two types of executive agreements—congressional-executive agreements and sole executive agreements.

a. Congressional-Executive Agreements Congressional-executive agreements are simply acts of Congress, ordinary legislation that enacts an international obligation by a majority vote of the House

---

[71] *See* Goldwater v. Carter, 444 U.S. 996 (1979).

and Senate, with the president's signature. Often, a congressional-executive agreement is resorted to as a matter of political expediency. It may be that there is a "blocking third" of 34 Senators who are prepared to veto advice and consent to a treaty. It may also be that a president prefers to submit an important international initiative to both chambers of Congress for maximum political effect.

Although congressional-executive agreements were first invoked relatively recently (in the administration of Franklin Roosevelt to pass lend-lease aid to Britain over the objection of a neutralist faction in the Senate), they have come to be acknowledged as a complete—and constitutional—alternative to the treaty power under Article II of the Constitution. Two recent congressional-executive agreements—enacting U.S. participation in the NAFTA and WTO—have raised objections that the original scheme of the Constitution requires important international obligations to be submitted to the Senate and to be subject to the supermajority vote requirement there. So far, however, no court has accepted such a challenge against congressional-executive agreements.[72] It has been suggested that congressional-executive agreements, as statutes, are permissible only for matters falling within Congress's Article I powers, whereas *Missouri v. Holland* (discussed above) holds that treaties (and statutes implementing treaties) can relate to matters outside Article I.

b. Sole Executive Agreement The second type of executive agreement—the sole executive agreement—does raise substantial constitutional concerns about

---

[72] *See* Made in the USA Found. v. United States, 56 F. Supp. 2d 1226 (N.D. Ala. 1999), aff'd on other grounds, 242 F.3d 1300 (11th Cir. 2001).

unrestrained executive power, because (as its name suggests) such an agreement is concluded on the single authority of the president. The ability of the president, on his own authority, to enter into international agreements with binding domestic effect can be derived in a number of ways. These have been specified in State Department Circular Number 175, first issued in 1955 (and since updated),[73] and have been qualified by the requirement that no matter what authority a sole executive agreement is made under, it must be promptly reported to Congress.[74]

For example, a statute or treaty (which would have been subject to congressional or senatorial approval) might authorize the president to enter into subsequent agreements, clarifying the details of an international arrangement. This raises relatively few concerns, as Congress is giving advance authorization for the sole executive agreement, and (in a sense) is delegating to the executive branch the power to make it. This would be no different from a congressional delegation of regulatory authority to an administrative agency. Likewise, the president is relatively free to make sole executive agreements if those pacts are *non*–self-executing and thus will require later congressional approval in order to be implemented into U.S. law.

The most controversial scenario for sole executive agreements is when they are made pursuant to the president's own, exclusive constitutional powers under Article II. These powers include the Recognition Clause, which gives the president the power

---

[73] Hearings on S. 632 and S. 1251 Before the Subcomm. on Separation of Powers, Senate Comm. on the Judiciary, 94th Cong., 1st Sess. (1975), at 279–301.
[74] *See* The Case Act, 1 U.S.C. § 112(b).

to receive and appoint ambassadors, and thus (implicitly) to recognize foreign governments, and the chief executive's function as commander-in-chief of the armed forces. Pursuant to these powers, the president can conclude sole executive agreements that will become part of the "law of the land" under the Supremacy Clause.

In a series of important cases,[75] the U.S. Supreme Court ruled on the constitutionality of sole executive agreements entered into with the purpose of resolving outstanding private claims between nationals of the United States and the government of another country. This type of agreement (usually sanctioned in some form by Congress after the agreement was already entered into) was typically a prelude to normalization of relations, and thus the Court held that these agreements were concluded pursuant to the president's recognition powers. In these cases, the Supreme Court held that the sole executive agreement was binding in domestic law, preempted any contrary state laws, and could even affect vested property rights.[76]

---

[75] *See* United States v. Belmont, 301 U.S. 324 (1937); United States v. Pink, 315 U.S. 203 (1942); Dames & Moore v. Regan, 453 U.S. 654 (1981).

[76] *See* Amer. Ins. Ass'n v. Garamendi, 123 S.Ct. 2374 (2003).

IV. Subjects of International Law

The "subjects" of international law are the actors in the international community that possess international rights and duties. Prior to the Second World War, only nation-states were considered to be "international legal persons," or subjects of international law. But in recent decades, international institutions, individuals, transnational corporations, and other entities have come to be recognized as possessing some aspects of international legal personality. This topic is an important one, since the viability of an international law claim often turns on the legal status of a particular entity.

A. States

1. State Identity, Recognition, and Succession

a. The elements of statehood The classic statement of the elements of statehood under international law can be found in the 1933 Montevideo Convention.[77] Article I of this treaty declared that "[t]he state as a person of international law should possess the following qualifications: (a) a permanent population; (b) a defined territory; (c) government; and (d) capacity to enter into relations with other states." And although this formulation has been criticized, the dominant view is that this remains the customary international law standard of statehood.

---

[77] Convention of Rights and Duties of States, Dec. 26, 1933, 49 Stat. 3097, 165 L.N.T.S. 19 (*entered into force* Dec. 26, 1934).

Two of the four elements—territory and population—are fairly straightforward and objective. Territory, which is the paradigmatic "object" of international law (something that is being *acted upon* by international legal players), is an obvious necessity for statehood. The Montevideo Convention requires only that a putative state's territory be "defined," but even this may not be a hard-and-fast requirement. A nation may have territorial disputes with its neighbors, and thus its boundaries may not be fully demarcated, yet that does not disqualify it from statehood. It will suffice that a country's borders are sufficiently definite.

Likewise, the fact that a putative nation's population is small or widely dispersed has been disregarded for purposes of statehood. As long as a state's population is a group of persons leading a common life and forming a living community, then it qualifies. Under this standard, the officials and support staff of the Roman Catholic Church of Vatican City qualify. But the World Court has indicated that even where a population of an area is largely nomadic, and thus widely transitory, that may still suffice for purposes of "permanence."

Aside from the population and territory factors, the most contentious issues of state identity arise from the last two of the Montevideo elements: government and a capacity to enter into international relations. These are often combined into a single inquiry of whether an entity has sufficient independence to exercise international rights and to discharge international responsibilities. Some polities have delegated responsibility for the conduct of their international relations to other countries, and questions have arisen as to whether they can independently engage in international relations.

b. Recognition

i. The politics of recognition An unspoken assumption in the criteria for statehood enunciated in the Montevideo Convention is that other nations are prepared to treat a particular entity as a member of the family of nations. Issues revolving around the recognition of states and the governments of states for diplomatic purposes have proven to be some of the most contentious in international relations. Unfortunately, the international law on these topics has been unsatisfactory, to say the least. The legal doctrines that govern whether a particular political entity rises to the level of a "state" are distinct from the question of whether the government or particular leadership of a state should be dealt with diplomatically. For example, no one questions that Cuba is a state satisfying all the Montevideo qualifications, and yet the United States refuses to extend recognition to the Castro regime and to normalize diplomatic relations. Conversely, whether Palestine can be said to be a state has more to do with resolving disputes over the nature of the political entity, its territory, and people, rather than recognition of a particular government or leader.

ii. Consequences of non-recognition Most of the consequences of nonrecognition of governments for diplomatic purposes operate on the level of domestic law, not international law. In the United States, at least, if a foreign government is not recognized by the President, there are two potentially significant repercussions: (1) its access to U.S. courts may be limited, and (2) the validity of its acts may be questioned.

Access to U.S. courts by nonrecognized governments can be affected in two ways. The first is that an unrecognized regime cannot bring an action as a plaintiff. The second is that an unrecognized government, if sued as a defendant, may not assert a defense of foreign sovereign immunity from the jurisdiction of the U.S. courts. If this seems unfair—that an unrecognized foreign government is barred from suing as a plaintiff, but can be freely sued as a defendant—a host of caveats and exceptions have softened these effects on court access.

The foremost exception is that the president (acting through the executive branch) must affirmatively act to bar a government it does not recognize from suing in a U.S. court. The government's silence in these situations is sometimes construed as a tacit form of recognition. Just as often, though, the U.S. government will expressly allow an unrecognized foreign government to sue private parties in U.S. courts. The bar against unrecognized governments as plaintiffs has also been evaded by substituting other parties as plaintiffs or assigning claims.[78]

Exceptions also come into play when an unrecognized government is sued as a defendant. The Bolshevik government in the Soviet Union was allowed by New York courts to claim sovereign immunity as a defendant in the 1920s, although it was then unrecognized by the U.S. government.[79]

Thus, a better statement of the rule of court access for an unrecognized government is that (1) if it seeks to be a plaintiff in a case filed in a U.S. court, it can be blocked only through affirmative action by the executive branch, and (2) if sued as a defendant, it will still be accorded foreign sovereign immunity

---

[78] *See* Upright v. Mercury Bus. Machs. Co., 213 N.Y.S.2d 417 (1st Dep't 1961).

[79] *See* Wulfsohn v. Russian Socialist Federated Soviet Republic, 234 N.Y. 372 (1923).

so long as it is regarded as a *de facto* regime. Likewise, the rule observed by domestic courts from most countries around the world is that the official acts of an unrecognized government will still be given legal validity, so long as that government has *de facto* control of the state (or part thereof). For example, the U.S. Supreme Court, after the Civil War, still recognized the official acts of the Confederacy (like the incorporation of businesses and celebration of marriages), as long as such acts were not, by their nature, hostile to the Union.[80] Later, in the long-running litigation involving the expropriatory acts of the Soviet Union in the 1920s, a New York court ruled that as a *de facto* regime, the Soviet Union's nationalization acts would be recognized, at least for real property situated within Russia and held by Russians (although not for assets located outside the country).[81] U.S. courts have also been called upon to determine the legal consequences when diplomatic recognition is withdrawn during the course of a lawsuit.[82]

c. State succession

i. Defined State succession occurs when there has been a fundamental transformation in the identity of the state itself, not its government. Such a change of identity can occur in a broad range of circumstances. States can break apart or merge into a union. Colonies can achieve independence. Parts of the territory of one state can be sold or otherwise

---

[80] *See* United States v. Home Ins. Co., 89 U.S. (22 Wall.) 99 (1875).
[81] *See* Salimoff & Co. v. Standard Oil of N.Y., 262 N.Y. 220 (1933).
[82] *See* Republic of Vietnam v. Pfizer, Inc., 556 F.2d 892 (8th Cir. 1977).

transferred to another nation. Understanding the precise nature of the state succession is crucial for determining the proper rule of international law. U.S. courts periodically confront issues involving state succession, and while they are obliged to follow the pronouncements of the executive branch in such situations,[83] the background rules of customary international law can be significant for their decisions.[84]

ii. Legal Effects The legal consequences of succession depend on the nature of the change in state identity as well as the type of issue involved. With respect to treaties, an important principle of international law is that a newly independent state begins its life with a "clean slate." In the case of decolonization, a new state can pick and choose among the treaty obligations of its former colonial master (although accession to any bilateral treaty will require the consent of the other treaty partner). The validity of the clean-slate doctrine has been debated in various fora, such as the United Nations General Assembly, but in the case of ex-colonies is generally accepted as customary international law. In the case of an entity that has split or merged, the issue of continuing treaty obligations is far more difficult. Practically, these problems are normally worked out by mutual agreement of the parties to various multilateral and bilateral instruments.

The public property and debts of entities subject to state succession reflect two sides of the same coin. The public property of a particular piece of ceded

---

[83] *See* Terlinden v. Ames, 184 U.S. 270, 286–88 (1902).
[84] *See* United States v. O'Donnell, 303 U.S. 501, 510 (1938); Ivancevic v. Artukovic, 211 F.2d 565, 566–74 (9th Cir. 1954); Barton v. Nat'l Life Ass. Co, 398 N.Y.S.2d 941 (N.Y. Civ. Ct. 1977).

territory can be seen as the "assets" of the transaction, while the debts (perhaps for public infrastructure) are the "liabilities." Not surprisingly, international law links them together. The nationality of individuals resident in territories subject to transfer or a change of state identity is also affected.

International law relieves a successor state of liability for the tortious acts of its predecessor. For example, a U.S. citizen was injured by a denial of justice committed by the South African Republic in 1895, but before the claim was settled, the Boer War broke out, and Britain conquered that nation. An arbitral tribunal held that the extinction of the perpetrator state terminated the international claim.[85] In other words, Britain did not succeed to the South African Republic's liabilities for international claims.

Contractual relations made by a predecessor state have been given very uneven treatment in international decisions. Some courts or tribunals have ruled that a successor state is under no obligation to respect the contracts or concessions entered into by the predecessor with private parties. On the other hand, the World Court in a number of decisions has ruled that a successor state is obliged to pay compensation if it decides to cancel the private contracts entered into by a predecessor.

2. State Responsibility

a. Defined The term *state responsibility* refers to the entirety of a nation's duty to respect the international law rights of other states and individuals and, when it has violated those rights, to make proper amends and reparations. In this broad sense, state

---

[85] *See* Brown Claim (U.S. v. U.K.), 6 U.N. Rep. Int'l Arb. Awards 120 (1923).

responsibility is at the core of all modern international law, and governs the manner in which entities may enforce their rights under that law.

b. Main issues While fundamental sources and principles of the international law of state responsibility remain fluid and dynamic, the critical elements of international claims may be summarized as follows:[86] an international claim, (1) if otherwise admissible, arises when (2) an act or omission, (3) attributable to a state, (4) wrongfully violates a duty owed under international law to another state or its nationals, when (5) it is the cause of the claimant's injuries, and (6) there is no justification or excuse for it. Some of these elements are procedural in character and may be regarded as the concern of the international law of diplomatic protection—i.e., the circumstances under which a state may raise an international legal claim on behalf of individual persons or business associations that are its nationals. The remaining elements are substantive in the sense that no assertion of state responsibility can be made without them.

i. Admissibility An international claim is "owned" by the nation making, or *espousing*, the claim on behalf of its injured national (whether an individual or business). The espousing state, rather than its national, controls the international litigation. More fundamentally, the espousing state can choose whether or not to bring the claim at all, whether to subsequently settle or compromise it, or whether to hand over the proceeds to the victim or pocket them for

---

[86] *E.g.*, Int'l Law Comm'n, Draft Articles of the Responsibilities of States for Internationally Wrongful Acts, available at <www.un.org/law/ilc/texts/State_responsibility/responsibilityfra.htm> (text and commentaries).

its own use. Although a handful of international claims commissions (including the U.S.-Mexican General Claims Commission established in 1923, the Iran-U.S. Claims Tribunal created in 1981, and NAFTA Chapter 11 Investment Dispute panels) interpreted their constitutive instruments to dispense with the espousal requirement for claims, the vast majority insist on government sponsorship as an element of the claim. Once the issue of espousal is favorably resolved, the next major question to be addressed is usually the claimant's nationality. A state may only make a claim on behalf of its nationals.

Another restriction on the admissibility of claims is the exhaustion of local remedies rule. This is premised on the notion that injured aliens at least should seek redress from local courts before seeking satisfaction through their own government's espousal of the claim under international law. If a claimant has failed to exhaust local remedies offered by the respondent state, the claim is normally barred. There are, however, reasonable exceptions to this rule. Claimants are under no obligation to pursue local remedies if to do so would be clearly futile, or if the remedies offered were not adequate and effective for relief.[87] The World Court has consistently held over the last fifty years that the rule of exhaustion of local remedies remains significant, and unless the requirement has been explicitly disavowed by treaty, it will act to render a claim inadmissible. Nevertheless, the Court noted in *Elettronica Sicula*[88] that the burden of proof was on the state wishing to show that local remedies had *not* been exhausted.

---

[87] *See* Finnish Shipowners Claim (Fin. v. U.K.), 3 U.N. Rep. Int'l Arb. Awards 1479 (1934).
[88] (U.S. v. It.) 1989 I.C.J. 15.

ii. Attribution Assuming that a party can show that its claim is otherwise admissible, the party must then demonstrate that the respondent state is actually responsible for the act that gave rise to the claim.[89] Such acts might include expropriations of foreign property or investments, regulatory interference with foreign contracts, or denials of justice. (States are also liable for their omissions, such as the failure to protect an alien's property from depredation.) Whatever the underlying wrongful act or violation of a duty owed under international law (considered next), the question is whether that conduct is attributable, or imputable, to the respondent government. The reason for the attribution requirement is that, under international law, host states cannot be the absolute guarantors of the safety of foreign visitors or the profitability of foreign business concerns.

International tribunals have consistently ruled that when any government official or agent engages in an act affecting the rights of aliens, even if that conduct is illegal or *ultra vires* under the laws of the host state, it is still attributable to that government.[90] Likewise, even though the acts of mobs or rioters may not normally be imputable to a government, if it is manifest that police authorities failed to take reasonable measures to protect the lives and property of foreigners, then state responsibility is engaged. In one notorious incident, the United States acknowledged responsibility for the lynching of Italian nationals in New Orleans in the 1800s.[91]

---

[89] *See* Underhill v. Hernandez, 168 U.S. 250, 254 (1897).
[90] *See* Way Claim (U.S. v. Mex.), 4 U.N. Rep. Int'l Arb. Awards 391 (1928); Kenneth P. Yeager & The Islamic Republic of Iran, 17 Iran-U.S. Cl. Trib. Rep. 92, 108 (1987).
[91] *See* John Bassett Moore, DIGEST OF INTERNATIONAL LAW 837 (1906).

iii. Wrongfulness Depending on the nature of the conduct affecting the rights of aliens, international law will impose different standards of care on host states. One historically common class of international claims goes by the name "denials of justice." These are claims arising in situations where the host state's law enforcement system or judiciary failed to operate properly, and, as a consequence, a foreigner's rights were affected. Such a case was the *B.E. Chattin Claim*, where the U.S.-Mexico General Claims Commission ruled that the procedural defects in the claimant's show-trial (including the failure to be informed of the charges, the lack of oaths for the witnesses, and the long delays) amounted to a denial of justice.[92] With the advent of international standards of criminal justice—often contained in international human rights instruments—a host state is highly likely to be held responsible for its failure to follow those rules.

Another class of claims involves assertions that a host state has failed to protect foreign persons or their property residing within its territory. In cases such as these, a state is being charged with an omission. The standard adopted by most international tribunals is some form of due diligence: a state is required to exercise the same care in protecting foreigners as it would in protecting its own similarly situated nationals. In the *William E. Chapman Claim*, for example, a claims commission ruled that Mexico had failed to grant the police protection for a U.S. consul (who had earlier been threatened by a private Mexican citizen) that it would for one of its own officials, and was therefore liable.[93]

---

[92] 4 U.N. Rep. Int'l Arb. Awards 282 (1927).
[93] 4 U.N. Rep. Int'l Arb. Awards 632 (1927).

B. International Organizations and Tribunals

Collectivities of nations, often called international organizations or international institutions, have become a notable feature on the landscape of international relations. Even so, international law was rather slow in recognizing the legal status, or international legal personality, of these entities. The story of this transformation in international law—recognizing international actors other than states—not only presaged the revolutionary idea that individuals could carry international legal rights and duties, but was also a significant advance for functional cooperation among countries.

1. The League of Nations and the United Nations

The dream of a universal international organization, aspiring to garner global membership and addressing a wide range of international problems, was first seriously attempted by the creation of the League of Nations in 1919, after World War I. The institutional structure of the League was to provide the model for virtually every subsequent international organization. The League "organs" included an *Assembly*, where each member of the organization had one vote, and which set the general policies of the institution, adopted budgets, and was assigned specific tasks for debating issues of disarmament and economic cooperation. Counterpoised with the Assembly was the League *Council*, a much smaller body in which the great powers had permanent representation and other nations had rotating membership. In addition to these organs was the creation of a permanent staff for the League, led by the *Secretariat*. The idea for this was that the institution could rely on a professional, international civil service that owed its primary loyalty to the League, not to individual countries of nationality. Lastly, a judicial entity to provide neutral decisions on legal disputes, the *Permanent Court of International Justice,* was established in association with the League (although, technically speaking, a separate institution).

When plans were made to launch a new international organization after the Second World War—the United Nations—the template and institutional design were already in place. And, indeed, the UN's organs closely tracked those of the League: a *General Assembly, Security Council, Secretariat,* and the *International Court of Justice* along with an *Economic and Social Council* and *Trusteeship Council* (the latter now defunct with the end of colonialism). As with the League, the UN's real successes have been in areas such as promoting human rights, spurring decolonization, facilitating aid and development, negotiating disarmament and arms control, and generally encouraging the rule of law in international relations.

2. Specialized Agencies and Regional Institutions

Today, the UN stands in the center of a vast network of international institutions. Known generically as "specialized agencies," their precursors were numerous functional bureaus and commissions created in various forms as early as the 1860s. For virtually every realm of human interaction—economic, social, and scientific—there is a specialized agency established (along the same lines as the organs of the League and UN) to manage cooperation, prepare new treaties, and draft needed regulations. In the area of international banking and finance, the "Bretton Woods" institutions of the World Bank and International Monetary Fund (IMF) occupy a central position. In international transportation, such agencies as the International Maritime Organization (IMO) and International Civil Aviation Organization (ICAO) make possible safe shipments of crude oil by sea and smooth flight connections (ICAO, for example, mandates that the international language of civil aviation be English). Likewise, institutions like the World Meteorological Organization (WMO) and World Health Organization (WHO) coordinate vital weather-monitoring and disease-prevention initiatives. All of this is a veritable "alphabet soup" of international cooperation across the broadest spectrum imaginable of global problems.

While universal, or global, institutions play a major role in international law-making, regional integration has also accelerated. Starting with the Pan American Union (now the Organization of American States) in the Western Hemisphere, such regional institutions have played a significant role in developing international law, especially in distinctive ways. Of course, the leading example of this would be today's European Union (EU), formerly the European Community or Communities. Beginning as merely a coal and steel trading bloc, it has evolved into a comprehensive economic integration regime, granting extensive competence to central institutions (located in Brussels, Belgium) for European economic, financial, labor, and social issues of virtually every kind. The European single currency (euro) is here, as is growing political, diplomatic, and security coordination.

3. The International Court of Justice

As was already noted in the context of tribunal decisions as an evidence of international law (see section II.D, supra), there is today a wide variety of international dispute resolution institutions. Some are subject-matter focused (such as human rights institutions, trade panels, and the Law of the Sea Tribunal), while others have regional competence. Some international mechanisms are available only for state-to-state controversies, while others are open to individuals and corporations. Of these institutions, the International Court of Justice still remains the most prominent for the resolution of international disputes.

a. Historical Background Proposals for the creation of an international adjudicatory body were first made in earnest at the Hague Peace Conferences of 1899 and 1907. In spite of the relative allure of *ad hoc* international arbitration, many states believed that international law would not truly be followed and enforced until there was a permanent institution for settling interstate disputes. It was only in 1920, with the end of World War I and the creation of the League of Nations that the Permanent Court of International Justice (PCIJ) was founded at the Peace Palace, in The Hague, The Netherlands. The PCIJ was conceived as a separate institution from the League of Nations, with potentially different memberships. A commission of jurists drafted the PCIJ Statute in 1920; although the PCIJ was eventually dissolved in 1946, the text of that effort is largely reflected in the current Statute of the ICJ. Indeed, for all practical purposes, the ICJ (created as part of the UN in 1945) is the successor to the PCIJ, and they are together referred to as the World Court.

b. Structure The structure and operating procedures of the ICJ are fairly straightforward. The current Court consists of fifteen members, each of whom serve nine-year terms. By tradition (though not by rule), each of the permanent members of the Security Council has a national on the Court. The remaining ten seats are distributed by region, so as to reflect as many of the world's legal systems as possible. Judges are picked in their individual capacity, and are not political appointees of their respective governments. Nominations of outstanding international lawyers from government ministries, law faculties, the bench, and the bar are made by members of another institution, the Permanent Court of Arbitration, according to nationality. Judges are elected when they receive a majority vote in each of the UN Security Council and the General Assembly. In addition, any party appearing before the ICJ which does not have a judge of its nationality on the Court is entitled to appoint an *ad hoc* judge of its choosing for purposes of the particular case.

c. Operating procedures The World Court traditionally hears cases in plenary sessions, with a full bench of fifteen judges (or sixteen or seventeen, if there are *ad hoc* judges appointed). A majority vote determines the case. (In case of a tie, the president gets to cast the deciding ballot.) Because the Court hears cases in full benches, the proceedings can be exceedingly slow, and it normally takes years before a final decision is rendered. Proposals to increase the use of *chambers* of the Court, consisting (usually) of five hand-picked judges to hear specific cases, have received mixed reviews. A decision of a Court chamber has the same binding effect as one made by the full bench, and (presumably) the same precedential weight (although there is no strict doctrine of *stare decisis* in international law).

Every matter that comes before the ICJ does so because of the consent of the litigants. The only question is how that consent is manifested. The Court does not—and cannot—exercise a mandatory form of jurisdiction over states. And only states may be parties before the Court. Article 36(1) of the Court's Statute thus provides: "The jurisdiction of the Court comprises all cases which the parties refer to it and all matters specially provided for in the Charter of the United Nations or in treaties and conventions in force."

i. Jurisdiction by *compromis* or *compromissory* clause The most common, and uncontroversial, way for the Court to receive a case is by the special agreement of the parties to submit it by special *compromis*. This is an especially popular vehicle for seizing the Court in boundary or other territorial disputes. When cases are submitted by *compromis*, the Court proceeds immediately to briefing on the merits since there is no conceivable jurisdictional concern.

An increasingly accepted way to invoke the ICJ's jurisdiction is through *compromissory clauses* included in bilateral and multilateral conventions. Such clauses provide that, in the event of a dispute arising under the treaty, the matter may be submitted to the Court. Although a compromissory clause need not be formally drafted, it must unambiguously indicate that the ICJ has been selected to resolve any future disputes arising under the treaty. Equivocal undertakings to have the ICJ settle a dispute are insufficient.[94] At last count, there are approximately 300 conventions with clauses that invoke the Court's jurisdiction. In cases involving compromissory clauses, the inquiry is usually limited to whether the dispute before the Court falls within the parameters of the relevant treaty.

---

[94] *See* Aegean Sea Continental Shelf (Greece v. Turk.), 1978 I.C.J. 3.

ii. Compulsory jurisdiction That leaves, as a final basis of the Court's authority, what is rather misleadingly called its "compulsory jurisdiction." This is premised on Article 36 of the ICJ Statute, paragraphs 2 and 3:

> 2. The states parties to the present Statute may at any time declare that they recognize as compulsory ipso facto and without special agreement, in relation to any other state accepting the same obligation, the jurisdiction of the Court in all legal disputes concerning:
>
>> a. the interpretation of a treaty;
>> b. any question of international law;
>> c. the existence of any fact that, if established, would constitute a breach of an international obligation;
>> d. the nature or extent of the reparation to be made for the breach of an international obligation.
>
> 3. The declarations referred to above may be made unconditionally or on condition of reciprocity on the part of several or certain states, or for a certain time.

Of the nearly 190 nations that are parties to the Court's Statute, only about sixty-two currently have made "optional clause" declarations under Article 36. Of the five permanent members of the Security Council, only the United Kingdom today accepts the compulsory jurisdiction of the Court.

iii. Findings of inadmissibility The fact that the ICJ has some basis of jurisdiction under the Statute—*compromis*, compromissory clause, or optional clause—does not necessarily mean that it will actually hear a case. Over nearly eighty years, the World Court has developed a number of prudential grounds for finding a case inadmissible, and thus declining to decide it. These grounds are analogous to the prudential reasons that U.S. federal courts often refuse to hear cases, even though jurisdiction is otherwise proper. For example, the Court will dismiss a case if its subject matter has become moot, as when in the *Nuclear Tests* case France unilaterally declared that it would no longer conduct atmospheric testing.[95] Although the Court was careful to say that it would remain seized of the issue (just in case the French decided to change their minds), the dispute was, for all intents and purposes, concluded. Likewise, the ICJ will not decide a case if the dispute is not sufficiently ripe, or well-developed.[96]

iv. Provisional measures Among other aspects of the World Court's procedures, it is important to note the ICJ's power to indicate *provisional measures*. These are interim measures of protection, designed to preserve the status quo between the parties while the proceedings are underway. For example, if the issue in the case is a border conflict, the Court might order provisional measures for a ceasefire and no further aggressive action to be taken by the two sides while the case is pending. The ostensible standard for the Court to indicate provisional measures is irreparable prejudice; in practice, however, the ICJ will often grant measures even when the underlying jurisdiction of the Court looks doubtful.[97]

The ICJ's power to indicate provisional measures has proven controversial. In recent years, U.S. courts have refused to stay the execution of Paraguayan and

---

[95] *See* Nuclear Tests, (Austl./N.Z. v. Fr.), 1974 I.C.J. 253.
[96] *See* Electricity Company of Sofia and Bulgaria (Bulg. v. Belg.), 1939 P.C.I.J. (ser. A/B) No. 77.
[97] *See* Aegean Sea Continental Shelf (Greece v. Turk.), 1976 I.C.J. 3 (Interim Protection).

German defendants who had argued that their conviction for capital offenses had violated the substantive provisions of the 1963 Vienna Convention on Consular Relations (VCCR) regarding consular access for criminal suspects. In each case, the ICJ issued a provisional measures order requesting that the executions be stayed, but the U.S. Supreme Court and relevant state officials declined to issue stays.[98] In subsequent proceedings, the World Court held (for the first time) that its provisional measures orders are binding on parties, and found that the United States had breached its obligation under the Statute of the Court to respect the ICJ's orders.[99]

v. Advisory opinions The foregoing has considered the World Court's contentious jurisdiction—cases involving states as opposing litigants. But many of the Court's most significant rulings have come in advisory opinions requested by an organ of the United Nations or one of its specialized agencies. Almost all of the critical decisions as to the "constitutional law" of the UN have come through the ICJ's advisory rulings.

C. Individuals as Subjects of International Law

The real revolution in the subjects of international law has been in the recognition of individuals as capable of both exercising international rights and

---

[98] *See* Breard v. Greene, 523 U.S. 371 (1998); Fed. Republic of Germany v. United States, 526 U.S. 111 (1999). *Compare* Case Concerning the Vienna Convention on Consular Relations (Para. v. U.S.), 1998 I.C.J. 248; LaGrand Case (F.R.G. v. U.S.), 1999 I.C.J. 9.

[99] LaGrand Case (F.R.G. v. U.S.), 1999 I.C.J. 9.

respecting international obligations. This development, standing alone, has been what has transformed a "law of nations"—the exclusive preserve of states, national interests, and sovereignty—into the dynamic international law of today. Persons are no longer the passive "objects" of international legal action by states. Nationality of individuals, as well as their duties under international law, will be discussed below. The substantive law of international human rights will be considered in section IV.A below.

1. Nationality

a. Bases Most nations in the world recognize either of two bases for acquiring nationality, or some combination of them. One basis for nationality is known as *jus sanguinis*. Nationality is transmitted "by blood," from parents to children. The other basis is called *jus soli*, "by soil," depending on the place where one is born. U.S. nationality law, which is based on the Constitution's Fourteenth Amendment, is centrally premised on the place of one's birth. That is why, for example, a child born in the United States of foreign tourists (or even illegal aliens) is regarded as a U.S. citizen. U.S. statutory law also recognizes the children of U.S. parents as U.S. citizens or nationals, even if that child is born overseas.

b. Statelessness Even in modern international law it is often functionally necessary to have an affiliation with a state. International travel would be impossible without the necessary travel documentation, including the indispensable passport (which is the ultimate proof of one's nationality). For this reason, the condition known as "statelessness" is regarded as problematic. Statelessness can be caused by the loss of citizenship, something that U.S. law attempts to avoid.¹⁰⁰ Classically, stateless persons were understood to live in a perpetual legal limbo, with no right of abode, no territory to assert as their home, and no right of protection from any government. International treaties on statelessness have been adopted in order to ameliorate this situation. Although relatively few states have become parties, national practices have eased, in part under the influence of developing human rights norms, which cover all persons irrespective of nationality.

c. Dual Nationality If statelessness (having no nationality) is a problem at one end of the spectrum, then at the other end of the spectrum, one must also consider the difficulties of dual nationality (having more than one citizenship). The most common source of dual nationality is birth in a *jus soli* country to parents from a *jus sanguinis* country, or birth to parents of different nationalities, both of which recognize *jus sanguinis* The combination of disparate nationality rules among nations can easily result in dual citizenship—someone who has loyalties to two states. It is possible for U.S. nationals to acquire dual nationality,¹⁰¹ and this has periodic bearing on diversity jurisdiction.¹⁰²

d. Tension between nationality and rights There is sometimes a tension between determination of nationality and determination of an individual's international legal rights. As the 1930 Convention on Certain Questions Relating to the Conflict of Nationality Laws provided, "It is for each State to determine

---

[100] *See* Afroyim v. Rusk, 387 U.S. 253 (1967); Vance v. Terrazas, 444 U.S. 252 (1980).
[101] *See* Kawakita v. United States, 343 U.S. 717 (1952).
[102] *See* Sadat v. Mertes, 615 F.2d 1176 (7th Cir. 1980).

under its own law who are its nationals. This law shall be recognized by other States in so far as it is consistent with international conventions, international custom, and the principles of law generally recognized with regard to nationality." This statement begs the question of under what circumstances a state may refuse to recognize the grant of nationality made by another country. In one decision, the ICJ ruled that states need not recognize a grant of citizenship by another nation if there is no "genuine link" between the person and putative country of nationality.[103]

2. Duties of Persons under International Law and International Criminal Law

The process of requiring individuals to conform their behavior to international norms—and directly punishing such persons (quite apart from their state of nationality) for infractions—has been ongoing for nearly 500 years. Even in the era of the "law of nations," where only states and their conduct mattered, individuals were recognized as subjects of international law duties and could be punished accordingly (as with the commission of piracy or the slave trade).[104]

The key moment for the imposition of international law duties on individuals was the Nuremberg trials of the top political and military leadership of the German Third Reich, held after the conclusion of the Second World War in 1945. In 1942, the Allied powers issued a general declaration known as the London Charter. The Charter specified a number of particular international crimes subject to the jurisdiction of any subsequently created international military tribunal. After the complete victory of the

---

[103] Nottebohm Case (Liecht. v. Guat.), 1955 I.C.J. 4.
[104] *See* Kadic v. Karadzic, 70 F.3d 232 (2d Cir. 1995), *cert. denied*, 518 U.S. 1005 (1996).

Allies in Europe in 1945, specific indictments were handed down for about twenty-four of the top German government, Nazi Party, and military leaders. The trials were conducted before a bench consisting of judges from the United States, Britain, France, and the Soviet Union.[105] The prosecution was led by Justice Robert Jackson, who took a nearly two-year leave of absence from the U.S. Supreme Court.

The German defendants raised a number of substantive defenses to the charges, at both the Nuremberg trials themselves, as well as the subsequent prosecutions in the courts of occupied Germany (these trials involved the financial, industrial, and judicial leadership of the Third Reich). The first such defense was the contention that every action taken by the defendants was an "act of state," and the individuals were, therefore, immune under international law. The International Military Tribunal (IMT) made short work of this contention, as the London Charter had specifically provided that "[t]he official position of the Defendants, whether as Heads of State, or responsible officials in Government Departments, shall not be considered as freeing them from responsibility, or mitigating punishment." The next defense raised by the Nuremberg defendants had also been anticipated by the London Charter. The defendants argued that as military and political leaders they had been merely following Adolf Hitler's orders, and were not culpable. However, the London Charter had specifically provided that "[t]he fact that the Defendant acted pursuant to an order of his Government or of a superior shall not free him from responsibility, but may be considered in mitigation of punishment."

---

[105] *See* International Military Tribunal (Nuremberg) Judgment and Sentences (Oct. 1, 1946), 41 AM. J. INT'L L. 172 (1947).

Nuremberg set an important precedent in demanding individual responsibility for violations of international norms. The trials were followed in 1948 by the conclusion of the Genocide Convention, which defined as a crime the targeting or destruction of particular populations based on their ethnicity or religion, as the Nazis had done in the Holocaust. Today, there is a long list of individual acts that are recognized as a breach of international law obligations. Some offenses—such as genocide, slave trading, and piracy—have been declared to be within a "universal jurisdiction," allowing any country to prosecute any individual.[106] Other crimes have been made the subject of particular treaty regimes, in which specific offenses are defined and then states promise either to prosecute the suspect or extradite the person to a country that will. This is known as the *aut dedere aut judicare* principle, meaning literally "hand over or prosecute." Aircraft sabotage and hijacking are respectively the subject of two separate treaties, as are attacks on diplomats (or other internationally protected persons), and hostage-taking. Most controversial of all has been the indication of terrorism as an international crime.

All of these efforts to create a broad structure of individual responsibility under international law and to eliminate the perceived impunity of war criminals culminated in efforts initiated after the genocides in Yugoslavia and Rwanda in the 1990s. The UN Security Council established *ad hoc* tribunals with jurisdiction to try persons suspected of genocide or crimes against humanity or grave breaches of the laws of war. These tribunals are currently operating and are

---

[106] *See* United States v. Hudson & Goodwin, 11 U.S. (7 Cranch) 32, 34 (1812); United States v. Smith, 18 U.S. (5 Wheat.) 153, 161–62 (1820).

developing a significant body of jurisprudence on this subject, especially as to questions of whether certain operations can ever be justified by military necessity, how far command responsibility extends to higher-ranked officers, or whether mass rapes of civilian women constitute a form of genocide.

The temporary and inevitably political nature of these tribunals concerned many states, and motivated suggestions for the creation of a permanent international criminal court. In July 1998, the Rome Statute of the International Criminal Court (ICC) was signed by many nations. (As of this writing, the United States has formally indicated its intention not to participate in, or cooperate with, the ICC). The critical innovation of the ICC is a permanent judicial institution and prosecutorial staff, standing available to commence investigations of suspected genocide, war crimes, and crimes against humanity (in essence, the original London Charter indictment counts). If a nation is unwilling or unable to initiate a prosecution against one of its own nationals, then the ICC's jurisdiction can be triggered.

V. SUBSTANTIVE ISSUES

A. Human Rights

Section Summary: The international law of human rights is exercising increased influence in U.S. litigation. Although the current position of the United States is that international human rights standards do not typically exceed protections afforded under the Constitution, such questions are sometimes raised. Additionally, the United States has become a leading venue for private civil litigation of human rights abuses occurring in other countries.

As already discussed, the Second World War marked the transition of international law from a system dedicated to state sovereignty to one also devoted to the protection of human dignity. This new paradigm was recognized in the Charter of the United Nations, signed by the victorious Allied powers in 1945. For the first time, an international agreement linked human rights with world order. Article 55(c) of the Charter calls for "universal respect for, and observance of, human rights and fundamental freedoms for all without distinction as to race, sex, language or religion." Article 56 calls upon states parties to "take joint and separate action in cooperation with the [UN]" to accomplish that objective.

1. The Universal Declaration

a. Background Shortly after 1945, the United Nations faced the task of pronouncing human rights norms. Its first effort produced one of the great documents of international law: the 1948 Universal Declaration of Human Rights. Drafted by a blue-ribbon panel of intellectuals and advocates (led by Eleanor Roosevelt) and with the input of national delegations, the Declaration is lucidly worded. Article 1 proclaims: "All human beings are born free and equal in dignity and rights. They are endowed with reason and conscience and should act towards one another in a spirit of brotherhood." Article 3 says simply and unqualifiedly: "Everyone has a right to life, liberty and the security of person."

The thrust of the Universal Declaration was primarily the enunciation of civil and political rights—those freedoms necessary for individuals to operate within a polity. The Declaration proclaims such civil liberties as freedom from slavery and torture, the right to recognition and equality before the law, freedom from arbitrary arrest and the guarantee of fair criminal procedures, and respect for rights of worship and expression. Also included are rights of participation in the political process. In addition to these "first-generation" civil and political rights, the Declaration also prescribes some "second-generation" economic and social rights. These include the right to work, rest and leisure, education, and participation in cultural life. Article 23(2) further mentions the right of everyone to "equal pay for equal work," the first mention of that concept in any document. Even though the Universal Declaration was adopted without dissent, it was not without controversy. Socialist countries were concerned about Article 17's enshrinement of the right to property. The United States was concerned about the First Amendment implications of Article 12's requirement that attacks against individual honor and reputation be barred.

b. Nonbinding The reason that the Declaration could be adopted by consensus, despite controversial provisions, was that it was understood by all not to be a binding legal instrument. Perhaps the first recorded example of a multilateral "soft" law instrument, the Declaration specifically indicated in its preamble that it was "a common standard of achievement," something that national governments would "strive" for through "progressive measures." The United States issued a statement after the Declaration's adoption, which noted: "It is not a treaty; it is not an international agreement. It does not purport to be a statement of law or legal obligation."[107] While U.S. courts make reference to the Universal Declaration,[108] it has never been held to be binding.

c. Evolution of norms Over fifty years later, virtually all of the provisions of the Universal Declaration concerning civil and political rights have come to be recognized as human rights norms in customary international law or in other multilateral instruments. Perhaps just as importantly, the high tone and moral authority of the Universal Declaration set an important benchmark in subsequent international discussions and negotiations about human rights.

2. Other Global Instruments

a. Binding instruments It still remained, however, to turn the aspirations of the Universal Declaration into "real" and "binding" legal instruments. This process developed on two fronts: through global treaties—often negotiated under UN auspices—aspiring to establish universal norms, and through

---

[107] 19 DEP'T ST. BULL. 751 (1948).
[108] *See* Zemel v. Rusk, 381 U.S. 1, 14 (1963).

narrower regional regimes. Among the global treaties, two of the most significant and broad-ranging are the International Covenant on Civil and Political Rights (ICCPR) and the International Covenant on Economic, Social and Cultural Rights (ICESCR), both adopted by the United Nations in 1966. The ICCPR has approximately 144 parties today; the ICESCR, about 142. Even so, the record of observance and enforcement of these agreements has been mixed. The ICCPR has been regarded as the more specific in its obligations and the more burdensome for governments. The United States ratified the ICCPR in 1992; it is not a party to the ICESCR.

b. The United States and the ICCPR U.S. ratification of the ICCPR was delayed for many years because certain of its provisions became intensely controversial within various administrations and the U.S. Senate. The United States thus took reservations to a number of provisions in the ICCPR.[109] Article 6(5)'s prohibition of the death penalty for those who commit crimes as juveniles was one such clause. The terms of Articles 17 and 20 (on reputational attacks and war propaganda) were deemed inconsistent with First Amendment speech rights and were also reserved. Some provisions were interpreted by the United States as being coextensive with rights already granted under the U.S. Constitution. The United States also declared that the rights guaranteed under the ICCPR were not to be "self-executing," or directly enforceable, in U.S. courts. Although many commentators and some states have been critical of this type of reservation (and the matter is now before the UN Human Rights Committee), it has become a

---

[109] *See* 138 CONG. REC. 57481 (April 2, 1992).

common practice for the United States. The U.S. reservations to the ICCPR made the international human rights provided for therein exactly congruent to existing U.S. legal protections; to the extent that international rights might actually *exceed* domestic standards, the United States entered a reservation, understanding or declaration.

c. Issue-specific conventions In addition to the Covenants, there is a body of global human rights instruments dedicated to more specific topics. The topic areas include the abolition of genocide, racial discrimination (including slavery and apartheid), and torture; forced labor and exploitation; the status of refugees; and the rights of women and children. These issue-specific conventions overlap in essence with the more broadly formulated protections granted by the ICCPR. Thus, many countries that have chosen not to become a party to the ICCPR have consented to be bound by these narrower treaties. By contrast, the United States, which is a party to the ICCPR, has ratified only a handful of these more specific instruments: the Genocide Convention, the 1926 Slavery Convention and its Protocols, the Status of Refugees Protocol, the Convention on the Elimination of Racial Discrimination, and the Torture Convention. The Torture Convention has been partially implemented in U.S. law by criminal penalties and exposure to civil liability.[110] The United States has also ratified a number of treaties involving labor rights and practices, negotiated by the International Labour Organization (ILO), a UN specialized agency based in Geneva.

---

[110] *See* 8 U.S.C. § 1231 (2003); 28 U.S.C. § 1350 note (2003).

3. Regional Human Rights Systems

Just as the end of the Second World War saw the development of UN-sponsored human rights instruments, so too were regional human rights systems developed. The first of these was in Europe, with the creation of the Council of Europe in the late 1940s. Under Council auspices, the European Convention for the Protection of Human Rights and Fundamental Freedoms was signed in 1950 and entered into force in 1953, establishing the first international human rights court and complaint procedure. In the Western hemisphere, the Organization of American States (OAS), headquartered in Washington, D.C., developed a human rights regime starting in the 1950s. (The United States is not a party to proceedings before the Inter-American Court of Human Rights, although it does participate in some aspects of the work of the Inter-American Commission on Human Rights.) Last on the scene, the Organization for African Unity (OAU) fashioned a regional human rights system in the early 1980s.

The regional human rights systems are a signal strength of human rights law. The extensive jurisprudence generated by both the European and Inter-American institutions gives substantial content to the general language of the human rights treaties. This is particularly so in very high-profile cases and in response to developments that are antithetical to democratic values and human dignity. The Inter-American Court took a strong stand against the use of "death squads" and the supposed impunity of authoritarian regimes during a dark time in that region's history.[111] At the same time, many regional institutions have

---

[111] *See* Velazquez-Rodriguez Case, Inter-Am. Ct. H.R., OEA/ser. C./No. 4 (1988), *reprinted in* 28 I.L.M. 291 (1989).

been moving toward recognition of new classes of human rights.

4. Derogation

One problem that is common to both global and regional human rights systems is what to do when individual rights conflict with the security and well-being of the state in times of crisis. A critical provision of the ICCPR is Article 4, which allows a state to depart from its obligations under the Convention, provided (1) it is a time of "public emergency which threatens the life of the nation," (2) the derogation is "strictly required by the exigencies of the situation," (3) that certain core rights (such as the right to life, the prohibition of torture and enslavement, and freedom of thought and conscience) are preserved, and (4) that notice of the derogation is communicated to other parties.

The derogation provision of Article 4 was essential for the widespread adoption of the ICCPR. States want to protect their freedom of action in times of emergency. (Indeed, even the U.S. Constitution contains a derogation provision—the suspension of *habeas corpus*—that was invoked during the Civil War and in Hawaii during World War II.) The ICCPR's provision is virtually identical to Article 15 of the European Convention, from which it was drawn. That clause has been construed by the European Court of Human Rights in a way that allows a "margin of appreciation" for governments to declare national emergencies but also imposes substantial restrictions on derogations. Thus, in *Lawless v. Ireland*,[112] that Court ruled that Ireland was justified in declaring an emergency in the

---

[112] 3 Eur. Ct. H.R. (ser. A) No. 1 (1961).

wake of Irish Republican Army attacks and that detention of suspects for limited periods without trial was "strictly required by the exigencies of the situation." The fact that these derogation provisions indicate that certain rights (such as the rights to life, and to be free of torture and slavery) can never be violated is perhaps their most important characteristic.

5. The Customary International Law of Human Rights

a. General examples The proliferation of human rights treaties does not mean that customary international law has receded in significance, given that many countries fail to ratify human rights instruments or may take decades to do so. For example, irrespective of their specific treaty commitments, states that have engaged in a systematic policy of abusing the rights of their citizens—including genocide, extrajudicial killing, enslavement, torture, prolonged or arbitrary detention, or racial or gender discrimination—are viewed as having violated customary international law norms. Moreover, certain customary human rights norms (such as the prohibitions against genocide, slavery, and torture) have achieved the status of *jus cogens* obligations—that is, preemptory norms from which no state may legally derogate, even by treaty.

b. The Alien Tort Statute and the Torture Victim Protection Act Through a combination of customary international law and a 1789 Act of Congress, the United States has become a leading venue for private human rights litigation by non-U.S. citizens throughout the world. The Alien Tort Statute (ATS) provides that U.S. courts have "jurisdiction of any civil action by an alien for a tort only, committed in violation of the law of nations or a treaty of the United States."[113] In a landmark case—*Filartiga v. Peña-Irala*[114]—the ATS was interpreted to mean that if a foreign plaintiff can show an injury caused by a tort "committed in violation of the law of nations," then U.S. courts could provide relief. The plaintiffs in that case had been victims of state-sponsored torture in Paraguay. They fled from that country, settled in the United States, and later found their torturer residing as an illegal alien in the United States. *Filartiga* has spawned a wide body of human rights litigation in the United States,[115] involving disputes as varied as Ferdinand Marcos' political abuses as former president of the Philippines, mass rapes committed by Bosnian-Serb forces in the former Yugoslavia, genocides in Rwanda, political oppression in Ethiopia, and arbitrary detentions of individuals in Bolivia and Haiti. What these all had in common was a showing that the underlying conduct violated international law. One notable limitation of the ATS is that it does not grant jurisdiction in suits brought against foreign states or sovereigns, only against individual defendants. In 1996, Congress supplemented the ATS by adopting the Torture Victim Protection Act (TVPA), which provided a similar cause of action to U.S. citizens who were victims of state-sponsored torture or extrajudicial killing.[116]

---

[113] 28 U.S.C. § 1350 (2003).
[114] 630 F.2d 876 (2d Cir. 1980).
[115] *See, e.g.*, Tel-Oren v. Libyan Arab Republic, 726 F.2d 772 (D.C. Cir. 1984), *cert. denied*, 470 U.S. 1003 (1985); Kadic v. Karadzic, 70 F.3d 232 (2d Cir. 1995).
[116] 28 U.S.C. § 1350 note (2003).

B. The Law of War and International Humanitarian Law

Closely allied with human rights law, the law of war and international humanitarian law are primarily concerned with ameliorating the horrors of armed conflict. This subject sometimes arises in the context of human rights litigation in U.S. courts.

1. Introduction

The outbreak of war between states does not in itself suspend the operation of international law. From the most ancient times, the law of nations has always included rules by which states attempt to moderate the effects of conflict and govern the conduct of hostilities. The law of nations was traditionally divided into two branches—rules governing nations in their peaceful relations and norms used in warfare. The laws of war, the *jus in bello*, were a significant aspect of medieval and early-modern state relations. Chivalry and restraint gradually gave way to the horrors of "modern" conflict, featuring total warfare, the involvement of large civilian populations, and the emergence of new, and ever deadlier, means of killing.

2. The Hague Law

The combined work product of the 1899 and 1907 Hague Peace Conferences on the laws of war is known simply as the "Hague Law." The primary thrusts of this body of conventional law were to regularize expectations by belligerent states as to how their enemies would conduct hostilities and treat prisoners of war and hospital facilities, and also to build confidence that certain kinds of weapons or tactics would not be employed in wartime. The critical underlying principles of the Hague Law were that unnecessary suffering and indiscriminate killing should be avoided in military conflicts (achieved through the abolition of certain kinds of munitions and delivery systems), and that military necessity was the benchmark for determining the proper restraints on hostilities. The United States has enforced such provisions, not only in reference to its own combatants, but also to enemy soldiers and commanders.[117]

The delegates at the Hague Peace Conferences also recognized that the laws of war were just at the beginning of a process of codification and clarification, and that customary international law norms remained significant. Included in each of the Hague treaties was the "Martens Clause" (named after the Russian international lawyer who proposed it), incorporating customary norms into the treaty regimes.

The Hague Law has spurred no less than three subsequent developments in the law of war. The first is the consistent use of international law to attempt to control and reduce dangerous or indiscriminate armaments and modes of warfare, with a particular emphasis on abolishing weapons of mass destruction. Some novel military tactics, however, such as use of submarines to attack enemy shipping, proved so popular that there never formed a universal consensus that the practice should be abolished. Likewise, although many nations abhorred the use of poison gas in World War I, few nations were initially willing to take the chance of unilaterally denouncing their use and destroying all of their stockpiles. Many states viewed the best deterrent against the use of chemical weapons to be that each side in a conflict

---

[117] *See* Ex parte Quirin, 317 U.S. 1, 28, 33 (1942); In re Yamashita, 327 U.S. 1 (1946).

had them and was prepared to retaliate if the other side used them first.

3. The Geneva Conventions

The second legacy of the Hague Law was a very different emphasis in the laws of war for protection of civilians, prisoners of war, and other noncombatants (*hors de combat*). After World War II—where civilian populations were targeted for destruction (if not annihilation) by belligerent forces and were particularly vulnerable to air bombardment, occupation, and enslavement—efforts were begun to negotiate a new thrust for the laws of war. The International Committee of the Red Cross (ICRC), a Swiss nongovernmental organization that had been earlier recognized as the principal agency for the protection of noncombatants in wartime, led negotiations for the 1949 Geneva Conventions for the Protection of War Victims. The four agreements included instruments on wounded and sick soldiers in the field, wounded, sick, and shipwrecked sailors at sea, prisoners of war, and civilians. The four conventions contained a series of common articles (including a form of the Martens Clause on custom), as well as very detailed rules and protections for the different classes of noncombatants. Together the Geneva Conventions are known as the "Geneva Law," or, more descriptively, *international humanitarian law.*

Although the Geneva Conventions have been widely ratified (including by the United States), serious concerns have arisen as to their application in certain kinds of situations.[118] For example, it is still

---

[118] *See* Kadic v. Karadzic, 70 F.3d 232 (2d Cir. 1995); Iwanowa v. Ford Motor Co., 67 F. Supp. 2d 424 (D.N.J. 1999).

unclear whether the protections of the Geneva Conventions apply only to individuals involved in international conflicts, as opposed to civil wars. In reality, civilians tend to be brutalized more in internal conflicts. Common Article 3 of the Geneva Conventions attempted to extend the reach of the treaties to civil wars, as later acknowledged by the ICJ in the *Nicaragua* case.[119] In a further development in 1977, two Additional Protocols were negotiated for the Geneva Conventions, and they apply its protections to most internal conflicts and wars of national liberation, although not to situations of "internal disturbances and tensions, such as riots, isolated and sporadic acts of violence." (The United States is not a party to either protocol).

The reach of international humanitarian law to encompass internal conflicts is exemplified by the International Criminal Tribunal for the former Yugoslavia (ICTY), established by the UN Security Council in 1993 to "try those persons responsible for serious breaches of international humanitarian law committed on the territory of the Former Yugoslavia." Continuing with the post-World War II trend of international law holding individuals responsible for their own acts, the ICTY has had the opportunity to clarify and apply the internal conflicts principle and many other aspects of international humanitarian law. (A UN-established tribunal for Rwanda—which shares the ICTY's prosecutorial staff and appeals judges—has also made important contributions in this regard.) In one decision,[120] the ICTY's Appeals Chamber rejected a

---

[119] *See* Military and Paramilitary Activities (Nicar. v. U.S.), 1986 I.C.J. 14, 113–14.
[120] Prosecutor v. Tadic, 35 I.L.M. 32 (1996) (ICTY App. 1995).

defendant's claim that the Tribunal lacked jurisdiction over him because his alleged crimes occurred in the course of an internal conflict, and thus were not covered under the Geneva Conventions, their Protocols, or customary international law.

4. Treatment of Enemy Nationals

The last bequest of the Hague Law was the clarification of the treatment of enemy nationals and their property in time of war. Although outright confiscations of private property have always been a common feature of military operations, international law has attempted to ameliorate the harsh effects of such measures. Even so, in the United States at least, the president still has exceptionally broad powers to register and control the property of enemy aliens under the Trading with the Enemy Act.[121] Such measures can extend to the supervision, or even the internment, of such individuals. The 1949 Geneva Convention Relative to the Protection of Civilian Persons in Time of War does, to some degree, restrain this kind of action.

C. International Economic Law

Questions involving international economic relations (including trade liberalization and investment protection) are increasingly being litigated in U.S. courts. These issues often turn on the interpretation of longstanding treaty regimes and customary practices.

---

[121] 50 U.S.C. §§ 21–24 (2003).

1. International Trade and Monetary Law

What makes the vast and growing network of private commercial relations across national boundaries possible is the global system of trade and monetary liberalization. This system has been the subject of treaties and custom for two centuries or more.

a. Friendship, commerce, and navigation treaties States (and their nationals) have always competed in the global marketplace, and have attempted to seek legal advantages and benefits. The primary thrust of this competition has been in the area of *tariffs*—import taxes imposed on foreign goods in order to make them less attractive to domestic buyers. Along with *quotas* (quantitative limits on certain imports) and certain qualitative restrictions, tariffs are the main tool of trade protectionism. The United States, when it has been of a mind to reduce protection and promote free trade (and there have been many periods wherein it has not been so disposed), has relied on a network of bilateral friendship, commerce, and navigation (FCN) treaties. These instruments extend "national treatment" and certain trade benefits to the other party, on the basis of mutuality and reciprocity.[122] FCN treaties are often combined with "most-favored-nation" (MFN) clauses, a promise that the United States will extend the same trade terms to the other party that it gives our most-favored trading partners.[123]

b. The Bretton Woods institutions, generally After the experience of the global Depression of the 1930s,

---

[122] *See* Sumitomo Shoji Am. v. Avagliano, 457 U.S. 176 (1982).
[123] *See* Kolovrat v. Oregon, 366 U.S. 187 (1961).

which was brought on in large measure by rampant trade protectionism in Europe and the United States, plans were made at the conclusion of World War II to create a new global trading regime. The original idea was to establish an International Trade Organization (ITO) that would serve as a central clearinghouse for the liberalization of import rules—that is, reduction of tariffs and quotas and other nontariff trade barriers. Delegates met at the Bretton Woods Conference (in New Hampshire) in 1944 and were able to fashion the two other critical institutions of a new economic order: the International Monetary Fund (IMF) and the International Bank for Reconstruction and Development (World Bank). Additional negotiations occurred at Havana in 1948, but the third leg of this new regime, the ITO, was politically unacceptable for many nations (including the United States). Instead, delegates negotiated an interim trade agreement, which later came to be known as the General Agreement on Tariffs and Trade (GATT).

c. The GATT, the WTO, and NAFTA The GATT regime persisted for over 50 years, until the institutional framework originally contemplated for international trade regulation was achieved with the creation of the World Trade Organization (WTO) in 1994. The reality is that the substantive trade rules of the new WTO are largely identical to those of the earlier GATT regime. That is why the world trade order is sometimes referred to as "GATT/WTO." The heart of the GATT system was simply a multilateral version of the most-favored-nation clause—all GATT signatories got the advantage of the low tariffs and other rules concluded during the successive "rounds" of negotiations. (These took the name of a significant host or personage, hence the Geneva,

Kennedy, Tokyo, and Uruguay Rounds.) With the establishment of the WTO, these negotiations to reduce tariffs, quotas, subsidies, dumping, other trade barriers, and abusive practices are now held on a regular basis.

The ultimate feature of GATT/WTO is its ability to fairly resolve trade disputes. This had been a constant criticism of the old GATT system, as trade abusers were often able to avoid sanctions. Indeed, to the extent that GATT attempted to avoid unilateral trade retaliations and sanctions, it was often unsuccessful. The new WTO has some institutional machinery to resolve this problem. Dispute settlement panels are available for expeditious trade litigation, with an appellate review process. The panel decisions are now binding and do not require political approval by the Ministerial Conference (where, previously, the trade malefactor could simply veto sanctions against itself). The extent to which WTO parties are obliged to change their trade laws in accordance with panel decisions remains unsettled.

GATT/WTO permits regional trading blocs and customs unions—such as those of the North American Free Trade Agreement and the European Union—so long as they do not act in conflict with international trade liberalization objectives. NAFTA—an agreement between Canada, Mexico, and the United States—has established dispute settlement mechanisms for a variety of its substantive provisions, including tariffs and duties for product imports and the protection of investments in host countries. NAFTA panels have held certain actions by the United States to be incompatible with its treaty obligations, and this trend may result in further involvement by U.S. federal courts in NAFTA issues.

d. The IMF The activities of the IMF have been no less important in their own way. The IMF's charge, under the Bretton Woods Agreement, is to provide structural guidance to the world economy by providing a multilateral system of payments among member nations and to eliminate currency controls and exchange rate regulations. The IMF successfully nudged national economies from fixed to floating exchange rates for convertible controversies. (This is what makes it possible to conduct most international business with a reduced concern for exchange rate fluctuations.) The IMF ensures monetary liquidity of its members by accounting for their available reserves, expressed in an artificial unit of currency known as Special Drawing Rights (SDRs). IMF regulations are periodically litigated in U.S. courts.[124]

2. International Development and Investment

a. Investment protection A number of treaty instruments and UN resolutions confirm that an important goal of international economic law is raising standards of living for all peoples in all countries. International law attempts to achieve this goal through a number of very different mechanisms. Promoting and protecting international investment flows is part of the international economic law of development. Issues in this area have already been mentioned in the context of state responsibility and diplomatic protection for foreign investment in a host country. The substantive standards of compensation for host state expropriations or nationalizations have shifted

---

[124] *See* Callejo v. Bancomer, S.A., 764 F.2d 1101, 1119–20 (5th Cir. 1985); Weston Banking Corp. v. Turkiye Garanti Bankasi, 57 N.Y.2d 315 (1982); Banco do Brasil v. A.C. Israel Commodity Co., 12 N.Y.2d 371 (1963).

over time. Some nations previously argued that expropriated foreign assets need only be compensated at something less than full value. More prevalent today is a form of the "prompt, adequate, and effective compensation" standard enunciated by the United States in the early part of the 20th century.[125] It is important to realize that there has been no multilateral codification of this principle of investment protection, although it has been enshrined in various FCN treaties and bilateral investment treaties (BITs).

b. Dispute resolution and ICSID Another institution that is available to promote investment is a centralized forum for the resolution of disputes between host states and foreign investors. Created by the World Bank in 1965, the International Centre for the Settlement of Investment Disputes (ICSID) in Washington, D.C., remains a favored choice for forum selection clauses found in overseas investment or infrastructure contracts. Its growing use indicates a desire by investment host nations to provide regular and predictable dispute settlement. Although some ICSID panel decisions have been controversial, it remains a respected forum. ICSID is currently used as one of the facilities for investment disputes under NAFTA and other free trade regimes.

D. The Law of International Common Spaces

International common spaces are areas or resources that are subject to international management and control. Law of the sea questions have been a

---

[125] *See, e.g.*, Banco Nacional de Cuba v. Sabbatino, 376 U.S. 398 (1964); SEDCO, Inc. v. National Iranian Oil Co., 9 Iran-U.S. Cl. Trib. Rep. 248 (1985), *reprinted in* 25 I.L.M. 629 (1986).

staple of federal court litigation since the early years of the republic, and international environmental law issues are increasingly being reviewed by U.S. courts.

1. Law of the Sea

The nearly 500-year history of the law of the sea can be reduced to a fairly simple dynamic: the conflict between nations with predominant maritime interests and those states that desire to secure access to maritime resources close to their shores. What has vastly complicated the law of the sea is that the identities of maritime powers and coastal states have changed over time, just as the range of possible (and permissible) ocean uses has vastly increased with technology and economic potential. Today, the crucial document on this subject is the 1982 UN Convention on the Law of the Sea (UNCLOS). Even though the United States has not ratified UNCLOS, it regards almost all UNCLOS provisions as customary international law.

Essential to understanding the contemporary law of the sea is recognizing the legal construction of maritime zones emanating out from shore. These zones matter; certain activities that are permitted by a coastal state within its territorial sea or contiguous zone (out to twenty-four nautical miles) are absolutely prohibited beyond that. Thus, the legal outcome of a law of the sea dispute could very well turn on the precise location of certain critical events. The closer to shore that a particular activity or resource is located, the more likely it will come under the control, jurisdiction, or regulatory authority of the nearest coastal state. Conversely, the farther one moves from shore, coastal state authority decreases until one reaches a point where it ends (called the "high seas"), and freedom of the seas—consistent with the rights of other states—prevails.

a. Internal Waters (IW) Internal waters are bodies of water so closely connected with a coastal state's land territory that they are assimilated to that nation's full territorial sovereignty. All maritime zones are calculated from what are called "baselines." Anything landward of these baselines are internal waters, and demarcation of the boundary has been a concern for U.S. courts.[126] The legal regime of IW is straightforward enough: internal waters are treated like the land territory. Thus, whatever sovereignty a coastal state exercises in its territory, it may exert over incidents occurring on its IW.

b. Territorial Seas (TS) Coastal states have exercised a narrow band of jurisdiction offshore for over 400 years. The essential idea has been that within this band of water, known as *territorial waters* or *territorial seas,* a coastal state asserts a form of sovereignty, qualified only by respect for the navigational rights of other nations. Historically, the breadth of the TS was narrow (usually three miles). Today, states may claim a twelve-nautical-mile TS.

The TS regime has always been qualified by the doctrine of *innocent passage,* which permits foreign vessels to freely traverse the territorial waters of other states. As long as the passage is "continuous and expeditious," and provided the conduct of the vessel is "innocent," access is permitted. Moreover, coastal states are limited in their ability to exercise criminal or civil jurisdiction over foreign vessels engaged in

---

[126] *See* United States v. California, 381 U.S. 139 (1965); United States v. Alaska, 422 U.S. 184 (1975); United States v. Maine, 469 U.S. 504 (1985).

innocent passage. International tribunals have traditionally ruled[127] that such jurisdiction can only be asserted when the passing vessel's activities have some connection with the coastal state or otherwise posed a substantial threat (as with drug trafficking), and this result was codified in UNCLOS in 1982. Coastal states were, moreover, limited in their ability to interfere with innocent passage, although reserving the power to suspend innocent passage for national security reasons. UNCLOS established a separate regime for passage through strategic straits, called *transit passage.*

c. Contiguous Zones (CZ) Under today's law of the sea, once one moves beyond twelve nautical miles, a subtle but important shift occurs in the nature of coastal state claims. No longer are coastal states asserting sovereignty (as they do in IW and TS). Instead, the basis of the claim is an assertion of control or jurisdiction over activities offshore, or (in the alternative) the avowal of sovereign rights to resources. Coastal state claims of control are usually made in the form of contiguous zones, which begin just where the TS ends.

The historic purpose of a CZ was as a remedy to the formalism of drawing fictional lines in the water.[128] The solution to this problem has been the assertion, by coastal states, of regulatory authority beyond the TS, in order to prevent infringement of certain kinds of laws within the TS or its territory proper. Today's law of the sea permits coastal states to extend a CZ from twelve to twenty-four nautical miles from shore, and most nations have done so.

---

[127] *See* The David, 1933–34 ANNUAL DIGEST INT'L L. 137 (U.S.-Panama Cl. Comm'n 1933).
[128] *See* Church v. Hubbart, 6 U.S. (2 Cranch) 187 (1804).

(The United States declared its CZ in September 1999.) Under UNCLOS, the coastal state can enforce only customs, fiscal, immigration, or sanitary regulations in the contiguous zone. Coastal state bids to enforce security regulations in the CZ were specifically rejected during the UNCLOS negotiations.

d. Continental Shelves (CS) and Exclusive Economic Zones (EEZ) Even though they developed separately, it makes sense to consider the CS and EEZ regimes together, because they are largely coextensive under the current law of the sea. The "continental shelf" describes a legal regime applied to the resources of, and activities affecting, the seabed and subsoil under the ocean. The EEZ regime governs resources and activities in the water column and ocean surface. Today, coastal states' continental shelves and exclusive economic zones can extend 200 nautical miles from shore (and, in certain circumstances, the CS can go out even farther).

Under the CS and EEZ regimes, coastal states are given two kinds of authority: (1) *sovereign rights* over the natural resources of the water column (chiefly fish stocks) and seabed (mainly hydrocarbons); and (2) *jurisdiction* over activities affecting those resources, including offshore platforms and artificial islands, marine pollution prevention, and marine scientific research. Aside from this grant of rights under the 1982 Convention, all other high seas freedoms will apply in a coastal state's EEZ and on its CS.

e. High Seas (HS) The high seas are all ocean areas beyond national jurisdiction. The high seas begin where states' EEZs end: at 200 nautical miles. International law over the last 400 years has developed a number of mechanisms to temper and manage freedom of the seas. One of these is the rule (like that of aircraft registry) requiring that all vessels have a state of registry, a "flag state."[129] The flag state has jurisdiction over all persons and activities aboard the vessel, which has sometimes been a contentious issue for U.S. courts.[130] The flag state is also charged with overseeing and regulating all aspects of the ship's construction, design, equipment, and manning (known as CDEM regulations), and ensuring that the vessel is in compliance with international standards. Most of these standards are set by the International Maritime Organization (IMO) in London.[131] Despite the prevalence of such "open registries" or "flags of convenience" as Liberia, Panama, and Honduras, international shipping safety is improving. Port states and coastal states have nevertheless sought to impose requirements that exceed international standards on ocean-going vessels, but this has been resisted.

Another mechanism for enforcement on the high seas is the *right of visit* exercised by warships. Certain activities are prohibited on the high seas and thus are grounds for stop and seizure.[132] These include piracy and slave trading, which are regarded as offenses within a universal jurisdiction. That means that warships of any nation may stop and prosecute individuals engaged in such international crimes.

---

[129] *See* Lauritzen v. Larsen, 345 U.S. 571, 584 (1953); McQuade v. Compania de Vapores San Antonio, S.A., 131 F. Supp. 365, 367 (S.D.N.Y. 1955).

[130] *See* United States v. Flores, 289 U.S. 137 (1933); Wildenhus's Case, 120 U.S. 1, 12 (1887).

[131] *See* United States v. Locke, 120 S. Ct. 1135 (2000); McCulloch v. Sociedad Nacional de Marineros de Honduras, 372 U.S. 10 (1962), *rev'g* 300 F.2d 222 (2d Cir. 1962).

[132] *See* Haitian Refugee Center v. Gracey, 600 F. Supp. 1396 (D.D.C. 1985); United States v. Romero-Galue, 757 F.2d 1147 (11th Cir. 1985).

2. International Environmental Law

a. Relation to state responsibility International environmental law began as a simple supposition, one that was intimately related to notions of state sovereignty: one nation should not use its territory to harm the interests of another nation in its territory. This is known as the *sic utere tuo ut alienum non laedas* principle (a notion that was significant also for the development of strict liability rules in Anglo-American law). This principle was adopted most famously in the 1941 *Trail Smelter* arbitration between the United States and Canada,[133] even though it was unprecedented in international law at that time. (The arbitral tribunal drew from U.S. Supreme Court precedents[134] as evidence of general principles.)

The most obvious, and lawyerly, approach to international environmental management is simply to make all the questions turn on answers of state responsibility. There is, however, a substantial division among international legal authorities regarding the relevant standard of liability for environmental harms. Language in the *Trail Smelter* arbitration is suggestive of a strict liability standard, provided that the damage is of "serious consequence" and the injury is established by "clear and convincing evidence."[135] The 1972 Stockholm Declaration also suggested a possible strict liability standard. But other sources, including the World Court's 1949

---

[133] Trail Smelter Case (U.S. v. Can.), 3 U.N. Rep. Int'l Arb. Awards 1905 (1941).
[134] *See* Missouri v. Illinois, 200 U.S. 496, 520 (1906); New York v. New Jersey, 256 U.S. 296, 309 (1921); Georgia v. Tennessee Copper Co., 206 U.S. 230, 237–39 (1907).
[135] *Trail Smelter, supra* note 126, at 1965.

Corfu Channel case,[136] might stand for the proposition that a state must be aware that it is causing environmental damage and fail to take steps to halt it, in order to be held liable for damages. This would be more consistent with a fault, or negligence, standard of liability.

Closely related to imposing liability and ensuring compensation for environmental damage is the developing notion of creating a separate international duty for states to consult and notify other nations about environmental issues and emergencies. Such a duty has been inferred from general principles and customary international law for many years. The 1957 decision in the *Lac Lanoux* Case,[137] for example, emphasized the obligation of co-riparian states to consult and negotiate in good faith concerning their mutual water resources.

b. Examples of international environmental regulation One defining characteristic of domestic environmental regulation is placing limits on pollutants or other environmentally adverse activities. Similarly, there are numerous multilateral environmental conventions that seek to establish such limits among states parties. In what is probably the most contentious cluster of issues for international environmental protection—preservation of the global atmosphere—internationally agreed emission controls have been commonly suggested as a way to combat acid rain (long-range air pollution), ozone depletion, and global warming (caused by carbon dioxide build-up).

---

[136] Corfu Channel (U.K. v. Alb.), 1949 I.C.J. 4.
[137] Lac Lanoux Case (Fr. v. Spain), 12 U.N. Rep. Int'l Arb. Awards 281 (1957).

In addition to quantitative standards for pollution prevention is the regulation of hazardous activities through permitting schemes. Typically an international convention identifies an activity (or range of activities) that might have dangerous effects, classifies those consequences, and then imposes review and permission procedures. A paradigm of this approach is the 1972 London Dumping Convention, which requires states parties to scrutinize proposed ocean dumping of different kinds of substances. Depending on which of three lists the material is found—"black" (prohibited altogether), "gray" (allowed, but with substantial restrictions), or "white" (allowed, with few or no restrictions)—a permit may be granted.

Another significant aspect of international environmental protection has been species and habitat protection. Beginning with the 1972 World Heritage Convention, states have been invited to establish internationally recognized wildlife habitats. The Heritage Convention (along with the 1971 Ramsar Convention on Wetlands) has states parties designate particular areas for international protection. These designations have been held by domestic courts to be binding on the host states. For example, the High Court of Australia ruled in 1983 that the listing of large areas of wilderness on the island of Tasmania, in compliance with the Heritage Convention, effectively blocked plans for a major hydroelectric dam project.[138]

c. Relation to international trade law One of the most potentially potent tools for protection of species, and of the entire environment, is the linkage

---

[138] *See* Australia v. Tasmania, 57 Austl. L. Rep. 450 (H.C. 1983) (Austl.).

of enforcement mechanisms to the global trading order. The first international instrument to do this was the 1973 Convention on International Trade in Endangered Species (CITES). CITES' solution to the rampant poaching of endangered animals and harvesting of rare plants was an economic one—remove incentives for profit by eliminating the trade in these items.

Today at least, the global trade regime has been bitterly criticized by environmental advocates who maintain that it unnecessarily restrains the regulatory actions of environmentally progressive nations. When the United States imposed import restrictions on tuna caught with insufficient regard for the safety of dolphins (which swim with tuna and are often killed when nets are thrown), the nations whose fishermen were affected sought relief before GATT institutions and, later, the WTO. In a series of decisions,[139] GATT/WTO panels have ruled that nations may not unilaterally impose trade restrictions on tuna caught with dolphins (or shrimp caught with turtles), nor may they unreasonably require heightened environmental protection (such as rules against certain fuel additives or hormones in beef) as a condition for trading in their markets.

One difficulty with this line of reasoning is that much of recent international environmental law has

---

[139] *See* United States—Restriction on Imports of Tuna, GATT Doc. D/S21/R (Sept. 3, 1991), *reprinted in* 30 I.L.M. 1594 (1991); United States—Import Prohibition of Certain Shrimp and Shrimp Products, WTO Doc. WT/DS58/AB/R (Oct. 12, 1998) (Appellate Body), *reprinted in* 38 I.L.M. 118, 174 (1999); European Communities—Measures Concerning Meat and Meat Products (Hormones), WTO Doc. WT/DS26/AB/R (Jan. 16, 1998) (Appellate Body), *available at* 1998 WL 25520.

been driven by the actions of environmentally progressive states, with the rest of the international community following behind. The WTO's requirement that environmental restrictions on trade cannot be imposed unilaterally, and must be made with regard to trade disciplines, may delay some needed environmental innovations.

E. Immigration and Citizenship[140]

International law grants wide discretion to states in crafting their immigration and nationality laws, but developing international human rights norms may place some limits on this discretion. In a few areas, treaties make specific provisions governing admission and exclusion of aliens. Bilateral and regional friendship or trade treaties provide examples, and U.S. refugee protections have clearly been shaped by highly influential UN treaties.

1. Overview

a. International framework An international system built on nation-states as key foundational units unsurprisingly recognizes broad national authority over the entry and sojourn of aliens. The U.S. Supreme Court held over a century ago: "It is an accepted maxim of international law that every sovereign nation has the power, as inherent in sovereignty, and essential to self-preservation, to forbid the entrance of foreigners within its dominions, or to admit them only in such cases and upon such

---

[140] The following section and the corresponding section of the bibliography were written by Professor David A. Martin, former General Counsel of the Immigration and Naturalization Service.

conditions as it may see fit to prescribe."[141] Similarly, international law generally accepts that "[i]t is for each State to determine under its own laws who are its nationals," although under limited circumstances other states need not recognize such a determination.[142] Thus most questions regarding immigration and citizenship turn on domestic law, not international law. Litigants today often argue, however, that international human rights norms, such as those protecting family rights or governing detention practices, have increasingly come to place limits on the broad state authority once recognized. Although such arguments have had only limited impact to date in court decisions, they sometimes carry weight in arguments over the policies of the political branches.

In a few specific areas, however, the United States has entered into treaties that unmistakably constrain national immigration decisions. Trade and investment treaties, both bilateral and multilateral (including NAFTA), typically set forth designated admission and other rights for specific categories of foreign nationals engaged in business. These protections are generally then incorporated into the standard regulations and administrative practices that govern temporary migration to the United States and rarely give rise to separate litigation. One other set of treaty obligations figures prominently in hundreds of cases each year, however—those that govern refugee recognition and related protections. Congress has incorporated those standards into statutory law, but courts

---

[141] Nishimura Ekiu v. United States, 142 U.S. 651, 658 (1892); *accord* Musgrove v. Chun Teeong Toy, 1891 A.C. 272 (Eng.).

[142] Hague Convention on Certain Questions Relating to the Conflict of Nationality Laws, Apr. 12, 1930, art. 1, 179 L.N.T.S. 89.

often consult international sources in deciding specific refugee law issues.

b. U.S. legal framework The basic U.S. provisions governing both immigration and nationality appear in the 1952 Immigration and Nationality Act (INA), as frequently amended. The INA occupies most of Title 8 of the U.S. Code. Those who wish to come to the United States, either as immigrants (also called lawful permanent residents (LPRs) or "green card" holders) or for a temporary stay (nonimmigrants), must first show that they fit a qualifying category and must then show that they are not ineligible under the inadmissibility grounds of INA § 212(a), 8 U.S.C. § 1182(a). Most permanent migration is based on family connections to a U.S. citizen or LPR. "Immediate relatives," meaning spouses and minor unmarried children of U.S. citizens, plus parents of citizens over twenty-one, may come in without quota limitations. Other family migration is numerically limited each year, however, and only family relationships that fit one of four family-based preference categories may enter. Employment-based immigrants must fit one of five numerically limited preference categories. Lengthy backlogs exist for the family preferences, but not, at present, for the employment categories. The United States also admits 50,000 persons each year for permanent residence based on a "diversity lottery," as well as a fluctuating number of refugees. There are twenty-two highly diverse nonimmigrant categories.

Congress extensively amended the INA in 1996, significantly tightening enforcement provisions—particularly those calling for removal of aliens with criminal records and, to a lesser extent, those applying sanctions against illegally present migrants. Congress sought to eliminate judicial review for most criminal aliens and a few other categories, but the Supreme Court's decision in *INS v. St. Cyr* declared that such persons retain access to the courts via *habeas corpus*.[143]

Congress also recast certain fundamental categories used in applying statutory provisions and possibly constitutional protections as well. Before 1996, the fundamental conceptual division was between exclusion and deportation cases. Excludable aliens were those who had not made an entry into the country—principally those whose qualifications for admission were questioned at a port of entry, or persons "paroled" into the country by INS when encountered at the border. (Parole allows the person to be physically present, but in the eyes of the law the parolee remains constructively at the border, no matter how long her stay.) Such aliens could be excluded for a wider range of qualities or acts than would result in deportation of persons who had "entered" the United States, and had access to fewer statutory avenues for relief from removal. Also, under the *Knauff* and *Mezei* cases, deportable aliens could claim due process protections, whereas excludable aliens could not.[144]

In 1996, Congress decided that this structure improperly rewarded those who sneaked across the border (entrants without inspection, or EWIs), for it placed EWIs into the somewhat favored deportable alien class. Congress therefore moved EWIs to the less favored side of the line. As revised, the key dividing line is now admission (formal authorization to enter following inspection by an immigration

---

[143] INS v. St. Cyr, 533 U.S. 289 (2001).

[144] United States *ex rel.* Knauff v. Shaughnessy, 338 U.S. 537 (1950); Shaughnessy v. United States *ex rel.* Mezei, 345 U.S. 206 (1953). *See also* Zadvydas v. Davis, 533 U.S. 678 (2001) (generally reaffirming *Mezei*).

officer) rather than entry. Hence EWIs are now inadmissible rather than deportable and potentially remain in that classification no matter how long they are present. But Congress still chose to retain a few provisions subjecting excludable aliens at the border to more severe measures than those routinely applied to EWIs; hence the law now distinguishes for some purposes within the class of inadmissible aliens. Entry marks that intraclass dividing line, now phrased as the distinction between "arriving aliens" (essentially those initially stopped at the port of entry) and "other inadmissible aliens" (meaning EWIs). Thus, today there are three relevant categories: deportable aliens, EWIs, and arriving aliens. Whether the changed dividing line has implications for constitutional protections has not yet been resolved. (For most purposes, statute or regulation provides significant procedures and the constitutional issue does not arise.)

c. U.S. agencies For over sixty years, the principal agency administering U.S. immigration laws was a component of the Department of Justice, the Immigration and Naturalization Service (INS). The 2002 legislation creating the Department of Homeland Security (DHS) transferred virtually all of INS's functions to the new department, effective in March 2003, but reorganized them to assure a split between enforcement and services. The Bureau of Citizenship and Immigration Services inherits INS's adjudication functions (*not* removal cases), including decisions on visa petitions, adjustment of status and naturalization applications, and asylum requests. Its director reports directly to the Deputy Secretary of the Department. On the enforcement side, the statute envisioned a single immigration enforcement bureau reporting to DHS's Under Secretary for Border and Transportation

Security, but President Bush later provided for still further reorganization. In January 2003, he essentially merged the U.S. Customs Service with the nascent enforcement bureau and then redivided the merged functions along different lines, creating two new bureaus that report to the Under Secretary. The Bureau of Customs and Border Protection (BCBP) now performs both types of enforcement (customs and immigration) along the border. It incorporates all of INS's border inspectors, as well as the Border Patrol. The Bureau of Immigration and Customs Enforcement (BICE) is responsible for virtually all interior enforcement, including investigations, detention and removal, and employer sanctions. The trial attorneys who handle cases in immigration court are part of BICE.

Decisions in removal cases have become gradually more formalized over the past fifty years. Since 1983 such cases have been heard by immigration judges who are part of the Executive Office for Immigration Review (EOIR) in the Department of Justice, a unit that has been separate from INS. Immigration judge decisions are generally appealable to the Board of Immigration Appeals, likewise a part of EOIR. The DHS legislation leaves EOIR within the Department of Justice.

2. The Application of Human Rights Norms

Nearly all human rights norms, including those of the International Covenant on Civil and Political Rights (ICCPR), to which the United States is a party, protect both aliens and citizens in their encounters with government authority. Hence the United States is bound to observe, for example, international norms of nondiscrimination, respect for family life, and protection against arbitrary detention in the administration of its immigration laws. The more significant question, however, is usually just how such principles or norms are to be applied in detail to such circumstances. Relatively few cases have wrestled with these issues, in part because of the non–self-executing nature of many human rights treaties as approved by the Senate. Four illustrative areas are discussed here.

a. Nondiscrimination International human rights law contains a broad norm against discrimination on any ground "such as race, colour, sex, language, religion, political or other opinion, national or social origin, property, birth, or other status," as phrased by the ICCPR (arts. 2, 26). Explicit racial distinctions would fall afoul of this principle, but the norm generally has not been found to require states to meet a high burden of justification to defend other distinctions appearing in their immigration and nationality laws.[145] Distinctions based on the nationality of the migrant (as distinct from national origin distinctions), by contrast, are widely accepted in international practice. Many states differentiate among nationals of different countries in applying both substantive and procedural provisions of their immigration laws, for example in deciding who must obtain a visa before traveling to national territory. Sometimes these nationality distinctions reflect disparate bilateral or regional treaty obligations, and sometimes simply different historical or cultural connections. Some have charged that disparate measures taken in response to post–September 11 terrorist threats, such as fingerprinting or monitoring requirements applied

---

[145] The ASIL study, THE MOVEMENT OF PERSONS ACROSS BORDERS 18 (Louis B. Sohn & Thomas Buergenthal eds., 1992), suggested that a rational basis test applies.

only to the nationals of designated countries, amount to forbidden discrimination. Nationality distinctions may not be used as a pretext to implement intentional racial discrimination, but international law does not provide detailed tests for identifying such pretexts.

b. Family life The Universal Declaration and the ICCPR declare the family the "fundamental group unit of society . . . entitled to protection by society and the State."[146] U.S. immigration law is generally harmonious with the right to respect for family life; family reunification accounts for over two-thirds of permanent legal immigration to the United States each year. Nonetheless, questions involving the right to family life can arise, notably in the context of deportation charges against lawfully admitted resident aliens who have committed criminal offenses. For many years, U.S. law had a provision that generally allowed individualized consideration by an immigration judge of family connections and other equities that might justify a discretionary waiver of deportation for a long-resident LPR in such circumstances. But the 1996 amendments greatly limited eligibility for such relief. Thereafter, some aliens have challenged their removal on family grounds and have invoked international norms as part of their case.

The most extensive international protections of this sort have developed under article 8 of the European Convention on Human Rights, which explicitly grants a right to respect for a person's "private and

---

[146] Universal Declaration of Human Rights, Dec. 10, 1948, art. 23(1), G.A. Res. 217A (III), U.N. Doc. A/810 at 71; International Covenant on Civil and Political Rights, Dec. 16, 1966, arts. 17, 23(1), 999 U.N.T.S. 171 (*entered into force* Mar. 23, 1976).

family life."[147] Several decisions of the European Court of Human Rights have applied this provision to forbid the expulsion of long-time alien residents (usually, but not always, individuals who first took up residence as children), even though the ground of the proposed expulsion was the commission of serious crimes.[148] State practice outside Europe, however, is far more accepting of the expulsion of long-time residents on the basis of crimes, even over objections based on family rights. The UN Human Rights Committee, set up by the ICCPR to monitor state compliance, has upheld such expulsions with respect to claims based on the comparable provisions of the ICCPR,[149] but the Committee has received only a limited number of cases in this realm.

c. Detention Detention is an inescapable part of the enforcement of a nation's immigration laws, and most immigration detention is considered a civil, rather than a criminal, enforcement measure under both U.S. and international law. Key international law limits on civil detention may be found in article 9

---

[147] European Convention for the Protection of Human Rights and Fundamental Freedoms, *done* Nov. 4, 1950, art. 8, 213 U.N.T.S. 221, ETS No. 5 (*entered into force* Sept. 3, 1953).

[148] *See, e.g.,* Beldjoudi v. France, 234 Eur. Ct. H.R. (ser. A) (1992); Moustaquim v. Belgium, 193 Eur. Ct. H.R. (ser. A) (1991); Berrehab v. Netherlands, 138 Eur. Ct. H.R. (ser. A) (1988). Other rulings have sustained deportation despite family ties. *See* KEES GROENENDIJK ET AL., SECURITY OF RESIDENCE OF LONG-TERM MIGRANTS 8–16 (1998).

[149] *See* Stewart v. Canada, 538/1993, Nov. 1, 1996, para 12.6, (UN Hum. Rts. Comm.); Canepa v. Canada, 558/1993, Apr. 3, 1997 (UN Hum. Rts. Comm.). *But cf.* Winata v. Australia, 930/2000, July 27, 2001 (UN Hum. Rts. Comm.) (finding that an expulsion would violate family rights).

of the ICCPR. It forbids arbitrary arrest or detention, requires that grounds and procedures for detention be established by law, and mandates that an arrested individual be promptly informed of the reasons for the arrest and have access to proceedings before a court to test the lawfulness of the detention. Most immigration detention falls well within these limits, but questions could be raised under these standards about some uses made by the Justice Department of lengthy detention on immigration charges after the September 11 attacks, particularly when limited notice of precise charges has been given or other informational restrictions have been imposed that could impair the ability to contest the removal or the detention. Although the ICCPR is not considered self-executing, the provisions of article 9 may be informative in deciding how due process protections apply in these settings.

d. Immigration procedures International human rights instruments contain few provisions directly addressing immigration-related procedures. The most explicit may be article 13 of the ICCPR, which provides:

> An alien lawfully in the territory . . . may be expelled therefrom only in pursuance of a decision reached in accordance with law and shall, except where compelling reasons of national security otherwise require, be allowed to submit the reasons against his expulsion and to have his case reviewed by, and be represented for the purpose before, the competent authority or a person or persons especially designated by the competent authority.

These procedural guarantees apply only to those lawfully in the territory and do not in terms cover clandestine entrants or those at the border applying for admission. Further, the article 13 protections, although important, are far more limited than the procedural requirements that apply under ICCPR article 14 to criminal trials. And even these limited guarantees may be overridden in part if there are "compelling reasons of national security"—a standard that may be of relevance in evaluating the use of *ex parte in camera* procedures in cases involving alleged terrorists.

3. Refugee Protections

a. Convention and Protocol Relating to the Status of Refugees Since 1950 U.S. statutory law has provided for withholding the deportation of persons facing persecution in their homelands. In 1968, the United States became a party to a widely accepted UN refugee treaty that establishes common standards for granting such protections.[150] In the Refugee Act of 1980, Congress amended the INA so that the key provisions conform closely to the wording of the treaty. INA § 208, 8 U.S.C. § 1158, authorizes the discretionary grant of asylum to persons who meet the UN definition (Convention, art. 1) by showing "a well-founded fear of persecution [in the home country] on account of race, religion, nationality, membership in a particular social group, or political opinion." Aliens granted asylum are entitled to work authorization, may bring to the United States their spouses and minor children, and, after a minimum of a year

---

[150] Protocol Relating to the Status of Refugees, *done* Jan. 31, 1967, 19 U.S.T. 6223, 606 U.N.T.S. 267. Parties to the Protocol are derivatively bound to the central operative obligations of the Convention Relating to the Status of Refugees, *done* July 28, 1951, 189 U.N.T.S. 137.

in asylee status, enjoy a clear avenue for obtaining full lawful permanent resident status.

Asylum is discretionary, but another section, INA § 241(b)(3), 8 U.S.C. § 1231(b)(3), implements the most important treaty protection, a mandatory protection against return to face persecution. (Congress meant this provision to implement the *nonrefoulement* guarantee of article 33 of the Convention.) The U.S. provision for withholding of removal states that immigration authorities "may not remove an alien to a country if . . . the alien's life or freedom would be threatened in that country because of the alien's race, religion, nationality, membership in a particular social group, or political opinion." Withholding of removal is country-specific and does not by itself provide other rights such as family reunification or eventual adjustment of status to lawful permanent resident, although persons granted withholding are normally also given work authorization. Both forms of protection, asylum and withholding, are subject to exclusions, by statute or regulation, which disqualify persons for serious crimes, past involvement in persecuting others, or dangers to national security. These exclusions essentially parallel equivalent provisions in the treaties.

In its first interpretations of the Refugee Act, the Supreme Court decided that the risk standard for claiming withholding is more demanding than that for claiming asylum.[151] To become eligible for asylum, an alien must show a "well-founded fear of persecution," restated in the regulations as "a reasonable possibility of suffering such persecution" if returned to the home country.[152] For withholding, the alien

---

[151] INS v. Stevic, 467 U.S. 407 (1984); INS v. Cardoza-Fonseca, 480 U.S. 421 (1987).
[152] 8 C.F.R. § 208.13(b)(2) (2002).

must instead show that persecution is "more likely than not." (To distinguish the standards in this way departs from the approach taken by virtually all other treaty parties, who generally consider that the same threshold test applies. Nonetheless the distinction is deeply ingrained in U.S. law.) In practice, a strong majority of asylum applicants can take advantage of the less demanding standard, even though asylum is discretionary, because the Board of Immigration Appeals has ruled that discretion in asylum cases should almost always be exercised favorably when such a risk of persecution is shown.[153] The 1996 legislation, however, expanded the range of statutory bars to asylum eligibility, particularly in a new requirement that aliens are ineligible for asylum (subject to specified exceptions) unless they apply within one year from entry into the United States. Because persons thus barred will be able to apply only for withholding, the difference in risk standards is likely to grow in significance.

The Supreme Court has also reinforced the nexus requirement appearing in both §§ 208 and 241(b)(3) of the INA, requiring that the feared harm be on account of one of the five specified grounds. It is not enough that there are general political reasons for the threatened persecution. The alien must provide evidence, direct or circumstantial, that the persecutor's motive for the threatened action against him focused on one of the five specified characteristics.[154] Later cases in the lower courts and the BIA have made clear, however, that asylum may still be based on imputed political opinion—opinion the persecutor attributes to the victim, even if inaccurately—so

---

[153] Matter of Pula, 19 I&N Dec. 467, 474 (BIA 1987); Matter of Kasinga, 21 I&N Dec. 357, 367 (BIA 1996).
[154] INS v. Elias-Zacarias, 502 U.S. 478 (1992).

long as the applicant provides direct or circumstantial evidence supporting such a conclusion.[155]

b. Convention Against Torture Article 3 of the Convention Against Torture (CAT), to which the United States became a party in 1994, contains its own distinctive *nonrefoulement* guarantee, forbidding return to a country "where there are substantial grounds for believing that [the returnee] would be in danger of being subjected to torture."[156] The Senate's resolution of advice and consent contained an understanding that applicants for this protection must show that torture is "more likely than not"—the same risk standard applied to withholding under INA § 241(b)(3)—and the implementing regulations repeat that test.[157] Most persons in such danger would also be covered by the refugee treaties and their implementing legislation, and anyone eligible for asylum under § 208 would clearly benefit from winning the more ample status protections entailed in a grant of asylum. But the CAT issue can arise separately in two primary settings. First, unlike asylum, CAT protection contains no nexus requirement. An alien at risk of torture for any reason is entitled to this mandatory, country-specific protection. Second, the treaty admits of no exclusions, not even for those who have committed serious crimes or pose a threat to national security. Many persons placed in removal proceedings after conviction of a crime are

---

[155] *See, e.g.,* Sangha v. INS, 103 F.3d 1482, 1488–89 (9th Cir. 1997); Matter of T-M-B-, 21 I&N Dec. 775, 777 (BIA 1997).

[156] Convention Against Torture and Other Cruel, Inhuman or Degrading Treatment or Punishment, *done* Dec. 10, 1984, art. 3, 1468 U.N.T.S. 85.

[157] 8 C.F.R. § 208.16(c) (2002).

ineligible, after the 1996 amendments, for any form of relief from removal except CAT protection. Hence the volume of CAT claims has grown significantly in recent years (exceeding 17,000 annually), but because legislation implementing this CAT provision was passed only in 1998, case law has only recently begun to confront many challenging questions of interpretation.

BIBLIOGRAPHY

This topical bibliography has been prepared as a guide for further research on international law subjects. The primary emphasis has been on book-length treatments and critical web-materials, on the assumption that researchers will have (relatively) easier access to law review literature on the Lexis-Nexis and Westlaw services.

For Further Research: The ASIL's guide to researching international law on the internet, the Electronic Resource Guide, is available at <www.asil.org/resource/home.htm>. The ASIL is also in the process of developing the Electronic Information System for International Law (EISIL), which provides a structured gateway to primary source documents available on the internet. A preview version of EISIL is available at <www.eisil.org>.

GENERAL WORKS ON INTERNATIONAL LAW

David J. Bederman, *International Law Frameworks* (2001)

Thomas Burgenthal, Sean D. Murphy and Harold G. Maier, *Public International Law in a Nutshell* (2002)

Ian Brownlie, *Principles of Public International Law* (5th ed. 1998)

Encyclopedia of Public International Law (R. Bernhardt ed., 1981–92)

Mark W. Janis, *Introduction to International Law* (7th ed. 2003)

Louis Henkin, *International Law: Politics and Values* (1995)

Rosalyn Higgins, *Problems and Process: International Law and How to Use It* (1994)

L. Oppenheim, *International Law* (Robert Jennings & Arthur Watt eds., 9th ed. 1992)

Recueil des Cours (Hague Academy of International Law)

Malcolm Shaw, *International Law* (1994)

(Third) Restatement of the Foreign Relations Law of the United States (American Law Institute 1987)

Marjorie Whiteman, *Digest of International Law* (1936–73)

<www.asil.org> (American Society of International Law)

I. Nature and History of International Law

Fontes Historiae Iuris Gentium: Sources Relating to the History of International Law (W.G. Grewe ed., 1985–92

Thomas M. Franck, *The Power of Legitimacy Among Nations* (1990)

Martti Koskenniemi, *From Apology to Utopia: The Structure of International Legal Argument* (1989)

John Bassett Moore, *A Digest of International Law* (1906)

Myres S. McDougal & W.M. Reisman, *International Law in Contemporary Perspective* (1981)

Arthur Nussbaum, *A Concise History of the Law of Nations* (rev. ed. 1954)

Religion and International Law (Mark Janis ed., 1999)

Oscar Schachter, *International Law in Theory and Practice* (1991)

J.H.W. Verzijl, *International Law in Historical Perspective* (1968–91)

II. SOURCES OF INTERNATIONAL LAW

A. Treaties

Douglas M. Johnston, *Consent and Commitment in the World Community: The Classification and Analysis of International Instruments* (1997)

Jan Klabbers, *The Concept of Treaty in International Law* (1996)

A.D. McNair, *The Law of Treaties* (2d ed. 1961)

Shabtai Rosenne, *Developments in the Law of Treaties, 1945–1986* (1989)

Ian Sinclair, *The Vienna Convention on the Law of Treaties* (2d ed. 1984)

Mark E. Villiger, *Customary International Law and Treaties* (1997)

<untreaty.un.org> (UN Treaty Index)

B. Customary International Law and General Principles

Bin Cheng, *General Principles of Law as Applied by International Courts and Tribunals* (rep. 1987)

Anthony D'Amato, *The Concept of Custom in International Law* (1971)

H.W.A. Thirlway, *International Customary Law and Codification* (1972)

<www.un.org/law/ilc/index.htm> (UN International Law Commission)

C. Other Sources and Evidences

David J. Bederman, *The Spirit of International Law* (2002)

Thomas M. Franck, *Fairness in International Law and Institutions* (1995)

Hersch Lauterpacht, *The Development of International Law by the International Court* (rep. 1982)

Mohamed Shahabuddeen, *Precedent in the World Court* (1996)

III. PUBLIC INTERNATIONAL LAW AND U.S. LAW

A. The Interrelationship of International Law and Domestic Law

B. Conforti, *International Law and the Role of Domestic Legal Systems* (1993)

C. Economides, *The Relationship between International and Domestic Law* (1993)

National Treaty Law and Practice (Austria, Chile, Colombia, Japan, The Netherlands, United States) (Monroe Leigh, Merritt R. Blakeslee & L. Benjamin Ederington eds., 1999)

National Treaty Law and Practice (France, Germany, India, Switzerland, Thailand, United Kingdom) (Monroe Leigh & Merritt R. Blakeslee eds., 1994)

National Treaty Law and Practice (Canada, Egypt, Israel, Mexico, Russia, South Africa) (Monroe Leigh, Merritt R. Blakeslee & L. Benjamin Ederington eds., 2003)

International Law and Municipal Law (G.I. Tunkin & R. Wolfrum eds., 1988)

Parliamentary Participation in the Making and Operation of Treaties: A Comparative Study (Frederick M. Abbott & Stefan Riesenfeld eds., 1994)

B. Treaties and the Laws of the United States

Louis Henkin, *Foreign Affairs and the United States Constitution* (2d ed. 1996)

National Treaty Law and Practice (Austria, Chile, Colombia, Japan, The Netherlands, United States) (Monroe Leigh, Merritt R. Blakeslee & L. Benjamin Ederington eds., 1999)

Phillip R. Trimble, *International Law: United States Foreign Relations Law* (2002)

IV. SUBJECTS OF INTERNATIONAL LAW

A. States

1. State Identity, Recognition, and Succession

James Crawford, *The Creation of States in International Law* (1979)

Hersch Lauterpacht, *Recognition in International Law* (1947)

D.P. O'Connell, *State Succession in Municipal Law and International Law* (1967)

Stefan Talmon, *Recognition of Governments in International Law* (1998)

N.L. Wallace-Bruce, *Claims to Statehood in International Law* (1994)

2. State Responsibility and Diplomatic Protection

C.F. Amerasinghe, *State Responsibility for Injuries to Nationals* (1967)

Edwin M. Borchard, *The Diplomatic Protection of Citizens Abroad: Or the Law of International Claims* (1915) (repr. 1970)

Ian Brownlie, *State Responsibility* (1983)

The Iran–United States Claims Tribunal: Its Contribution to the Law of State Responsibility (Richard B. Lillich, Daniel Barstow Magraw, & David J. Bederman eds., 1998)

International Law of State Responsibility for Injuries to Aliens (Richard B. Lillich ed., 1983)

B. International Organizations and Tribunals

C.F. Amerasinghe, *The Law of the International Civil Service as Applied by International Administrative Tribunals* (1988)

D.W. Bowett, *The Law of International Institutions* (4th ed. 1982)

Charter of the United Nations: A Commentary (Bruno Simma ed., 1995)

E. Osmanzyk, *Encyclopedia of the United Nations and International Organizations* (2d ed. 1990)

United Nations: Law, Policies and Practice (Rudiger Wolfrum ed., 1995)

<www.un.org> (UN main Web site)

<www.pict-pcti.org> (The Project on International Courts and Tribunals)

C. Individuals in International Law

R. Donner, *The Regulation of Nationality in International Law* (2d ed. 1994)

International Criminal Law (M. Cherif Bassiouni ed., 1998)

C.A. Norgaard, *The Position of the Individual in International Law* (1962)

V. SUBSTANTIVE ISSUES

A. Human Rights

Basic Documents on Human Rights (Ian Brownlie ed., 3d ed. 1992)

M.J. Bossuyt, *Guide to the 'Travaux Préparatoires' of the International Covenant on Civil and Political Rights* (1987)

Antonio Cassese, *Human Rights in a Changing World* (1990)

S. Davidson, *The Inter-American Court of Human Rights* (1992)

Guide to International Human Rights Practice (Hurst Hannum ed., 3d ed. 1999)

David J. Harris, M. O'Boyle, & Colin Warbrick, *Law of the European Convention on Human Rights* (1995)

Dominic McGoldrick, *Human Rights Committee: Its Role in the Development of the International Covenant on Civil and Political Rights* (1991)

J.G. Merrills, *The Development of International Law by the European Court of Human Rights* (2d ed. 1993)

Henry J. Steiner & Philip Alston, *International Human Rights in Context* (1996)

Beth Stephens & Michael Ratner, *International Human Rights Litigation in U.S. Courts* (1996)

A Systematic Guide to the Case Law of the European Court of Human Rights, 1960–1994 (P. Kempees ed., 1996)

The United Nations and Human Rights: A Critical Appraisal (P. Alston ed., 1992)

<www1.umn.edu/humanrts> (Human Rights Library)

B. International Humanitarian Law

1. Control of Armed Conflict

Ian Brownlie, *International Law and the Use of Force* (1963)

Yoram Dinstein, *War, Aggression and Self-Defence* (2d ed. 1994)

Louis Henkin, *Right v. Might: International Law and the Use of Force* (2d ed. 1991)

Law and Force in the New International Order (Lori Damrosch & David J. Scheffer eds., 1992)

John Norton Moore, *Law and Civil War in the Modern World* (1974)

Sean D. Murphy, *Humanitarian Intervention: The United Nations in an Evolving World Order* (1996)

Fernando R. Tesón, *Humanitarian Intervention: An Inquiry into Law and Morality* (2d ed. 1997)

United Nations Legal Order (Oscar Schachter & Christopher C. Joyner eds., 1995)

2. Law of War

M. Cherif Bassiouni, *Crimes Against Humanity in International Criminal Law* (1999)

E. Benevisti, *The International Law of Occupation* (1993)

Documents on the Laws of War (A. Roberts & R. Guelff eds., 4th ed. 1999)

L.C. Green, *The Contemporary Law of Armed Conflict* (1993)

F. Kalshoven, *Constraints on the Waging of War* (1987)

Virginia Morris & Michael P. Scharf, *An Insider's Guide to the International Criminal Tribunal for the Former Yugoslavia* (1995)

The Statute of the International Criminal Court: A Documentary History (M. Cherif Bassiouni ed., 1998)

Theodor Meron, *Henry's Wars and Shakespeare's Laws: Perspectives on the Law of War in the Later Middle Ages* (1993)

Theodor Meron, *Human Rights in Internal Strife: Their International Protection* (1987)

San Remo Manual on International Law Applicable to Armed Conflicts at Sea (L. Doswald-Beck ed., 1995)

<www.un.org/icty> (International Criminal Tribunal for the former Yugoslavia)

<www.un.org/law/icc/index.html> (International Criminal Court)

C. International Economic Law

Hazel Fox, *International Economic Law and Developing Countries* (1992)

F.V. Garcia-Amador, *The Emerging International Law of Development* (1990)

Robert Hudec, *The GATT Legal System and World Trade Diplomacy* (2d ed. 1990)

Robert Hudec, *Enforcing International Trade Law: The Evolution of the Modern GATT Legal System* (1993)

John H. Jackson & W.J. Davey, *International Economic Relations* (2d ed. 1989)

David Palmeter & Petros C. Mavroidis, *Dispute Settlement in the World Trade Organization: Practice and Procedure* (1999)

Ignaz Seidl-Hohenveldern, *International Economic Law* (2d ed. 1992)

<www.wto.org/wto/dispute/dispute.htm> (World Trade Organization dispute panels)

D. The Law of International Common Spaces

1. Law of the Sea

R.P. Anand, *Origin and Development of the Law of the Sea* (1983)

E.D. Brown, *The International Law of the Sea* (1992)

R.R. Churchill & A.V. Lowe, *The Law of the Sea* (2d ed. 1988)

United Nations Convention on the Law of the Sea, 1982: A Commentary (Myron H. Nordquist ed., 1985–97)

D.P. O'Connell, *The International Law of the Sea* (1982–84)

<www.un.org/Depts/los/index.htm> (UN site on oceans law)

2. International Environmental Law

Basis Documents on International Environmental Law (H. Hohmann ed., 3d ed. 1992)

P.W. Birnie & A. Boyle, *International Law and the Environment* (1992)

International Environmental Law: Multilateral Treaties (W.E. Burhenne ed., 1996)

Alexandre Kiss & Dinah Shelton, *International Environmental Law* (1991)

Ved Nanda, *International Environmental Law and Policy* (1995)

Philippe Sands, *Principles of International Environmental Law* (1995)

Edith Brown Weiss, *In Fairness to Future Generations: International Law, Common Patrimony, and Intergenerational Equity* (1989)

3. State Territory and Common Areas

Y.Z. Blum, *Historic Titles in International Law* (1965)

Q.C. Christol, *Space Law: Past, Present and Future* (1991)

P.S. Dempsey, *Law and Foreign Policy in International Aviation* (1987)

R.Y. Jennings, *The Acquisition of Territory in International Law* (1962)

Christopher C. Joyner, *Antarctica and the Law of the Sea* (1992)

Donald R. Rothwell, *The Polar Regions and the Development of International Law* (1996)

E. Immigration and Citizenship

Thomas Alexander Aleinikoff, David A. Martin, & Hiroshi Motomura, *Immigration and Citizenship: Process and Policy* (5th ed. 2003)

Robert C. Divine, *Immigration Practice* (2002 ed.)

Guy S. Goodwin-Gill, *International Law and the Movement of Persons Between States* (1978)

Guy S. Goodwin-Gill, *The Refugee in International Law* (1983)

Charles Gordon, Stanley Mailman, & Stephen Yale-Loehr, *Immigration Law and Procedure* (rev. ed. 2002 (looseleaf))

James C. Hathaway, *The Law of Refugee Status* (1991)

The Movement of Persons Across Borders (Louis B. Sohn & Thomas Buergenthal eds., 1992) (ASIL Studies in Transnational Legal Policy)

Richard Plender, *International Migration Law* (2d rev. ed. 1988) and the accompanying *Basic Documents on International Migration Law*

Rights and Duties of Dual Nationals: Evolution and Prospects (David A. Martin & Kay Hailbronner eds., 2002)

V. Miscellaneous Issues

A. Jurisdiction

J.-G. Castel, *Extraterritoriality in International Trade* (1988)

The Extraterritorial Application of National Laws (Dieter Lange & Gary Born eds., 1987)

B. Jurisdictional Immunities

Peter H.F. Bekker, *The Legal Position of Intergovernmental Organizations* (1994)

Joseph W. Dellapenna, *Suing Foreign Governments and Their Corporations* (2d ed. 2002)

E. Denza, *Diplomatic Law: Commentary on the Vienna Convention on Diplomatic Relations* (2d ed. 1998)

R. Jennings, *The Place of the Jurisdictional Immunity of States in International and Municipal Law* (1987)

Satow's Guide to Diplomatic Practice (L. Gore-Booth ed., 6th ed. 1988)

Christoph Schreuer, *State Immunity: Some Recent Developments* (1988)

B. Sen, *A Diplomat's Handbook of International Law and Practice* (3d ed. 1988)

C. Countermeasures

O.Y. Elagab, *The Legality of Non-Forcible Countermeasures in International Law* (1988)

Elizabeth Zoller, *Peacetime Unilateral Remedies: An Analysis of Countermeasures* (1984)

D. Peaceful Settlement of Disputes

Charles N. Brower & Jason D. Brueschke, *The Iran–United States Claims Tribunal* (1998)

Fact-Finding Before International Tribunals (R. Lillich ed., 1992)

G.C. Fitzmaurice, *Law and Practice of the International Court of Justice* (1986)

Christine Gray, *Judicial Remedies in International Law* (1990)

International Courts for the Twenty-First Century (Mark Janis ed., 1992)

E.D. McWhinney, *Judicial Settlement of International Disputes* (1991)

J.G. Merrills, *International Dispute Settlement* (3d ed. 1998)

W.M. Reisman, *Systems of Control in International Adjudication and Arbitration: Breakdown and Repair* (1992)

Shabtai Rosenne, *The Law and Practice of the International Court, 1920–1996* (1997)

Nagendra Singh, *The Role and Record of the International Court of Justice* (1989)

Stephen M. Schwebel, *International Arbitration: Three Salient Problems* (1987)

A.M. Stuyt, *Survey of International Arbitrations, 1794–1989* (1990)

Stephen Toope, *Mixed International Arbitration* (1990)

<www.icj-cij.org> (International Court of Justice)

<www.pict-pcti.org> (The Project on International Courts and Tribunals)